CONTENTS

How to Complete Your UCAS Application

This 19th edition published in 2007 by Trotman, an imprint of Crimson
Publishing, Richmond, Surrey TW9 2ND

© Trotman 2007

Editorial and Publishing Team
Updated and edited by Ian Turner
Editorial Mina Patria, Publishing Director; Jo Jacomb, Editorial Manager;
Jessica Spencer, Development Editor; Ian Turner, Production Editor
Production John O'Toole, Operations Manager;
Jaqui Palmer, Art Director; Tom Hulatt, Junior Designer;
Lorcan Mulligan, Production Controller
Advertising Sarah Talbot, Advertising Manager (020 8334 1617)

British Library Cataloguing in Publication Data
A catalogue record for this book is available from the British Library

ISBN 978 1 84455 126 2

Typeset by Ian Turner

Printed and bound in Great Britain by Creative Print & Design (Wales) Ltd

FOREWORD

WHERE DO YOU WANT TO BE IN THE FUTURE?

Now that you are about to embark on an exciting journey that will shape your future, the thought of having to decide what and where to study can often seem a daunting task. At UCAS we pride ourselves on our ability to help you make one of the most important decisions of your life.

Higher education offers a diverse range of courses and institutions, with opportunities for personal and professional development and achievement. Getting the most out of higher education and choosing a university or college you will enjoy studying at requires thorough research. Although research may seem like an extra chore to fit in between studying and doing your exams, think of it as an exciting opportunity for you to discover what is available to you. You may find that there are courses or places to study you never knew about, places that could possibly provide your perfect course. By researching your options you will make sure that nothing comes as an unexpected surprise – for instance, some subjects require you to take an admissions test.

If you are undecided about which course to study or which university or college to attend, go to www.ucas.com where you will find the Stamford Test. This short questionnaire is an easy and accessible way to match your interests and abilities to possible higher education subjects. Many students have found this extremely helpful when trying to make up their minds. But this, on its own, is not sufficient! Researching universities or colleges that will suit you academically and personally can take time if you are to find the right fit. It would be wise to spend some time attending institution open days and talking to current students, so that you can get a feel for what it would be like to live and study there.

Once you have some idea of the area you would like to study, you can use Course Search at www.ucas.com to look for courses in your subject. Course Search also includes information on fees, bursaries and other financial support.

Students can also register for the UCAS Card at www.ucas.com/ucascard. UCAS Card holders will benefit from getting regular advice on all aspects of higher education, help with their application process, tailored information on courses and institutions, profiles and insights into student life and special offers and entertainment. With this card you will have more access to information about higher education which can help you research your options.

You owe it to yourself to make the best of what you have to offer, so planning your UCAS application is essential. Your application is the gateway to your graduate career, so providing a strong personal statement will help you stand out in a crowd of fellow applicants and gain the right place. Applying for higher education via www.ucas.com has never been easier. The online application is clear and simple to complete, but help is always at hand online or from our team of telephone advisers should you need it.

There are many factors that should be considered when making your choices, but equally there are many sources of help at hand. The information in this book should help guide you through the application process itself.

On behalf of UCAS, may I wish you every success for the future.

Anthony McClaran
Chief Executive, UCAS

INTRODUCTION

This book is intended to be a guide for anyone wanting to gain a place on a UK higher education course. Last year, 390,890 people were accepted onto 28,900 courses of higher education at over 300 UK universities and colleges, and it is expected that around half a million individuals will apply for entry in 2008. All these potential higher education students complete UCAS applications in order to gain their university and college places.

THE JOB OF UCAS

UCAS (the Universities and Colleges Admissions Service) acts as the intermediary between applicants and their intended institutions of higher education, providing lists of available courses and means by which prospective students can apply for them. With very few exceptions, every application to a higher education course (whether for a full- or part-time course, leading to a degree, foundation degree, Higher National Diploma or Diploma of Higher Education) must be made through UCAS.

UCAS controls and monitors the flow of applications to institutions and their replies to would-be entrants. Each year, UCAS regulates the whole business of filling places on higher education courses by ensuring that every applicant is treated in the same way, and that all applications are given equal consideration by university admissions tutors.

UCAS offers a considerable amount of help to higher education applicants via its website, www.ucas.com, where you can:

- Research courses offered by different higher education institutions using a number of variables such as: qualification (degree or HND etc), subject, university or college, or geographical area.
- Link to every higher education institution's website to obtain detailed information on courses: their content, mode of delivery and method of assessment, as well as the qualifications and grades (or tariff points) and any additional requirements for entry (located in the course entry profiles).
- Make an online application to your chosen university courses through Apply.
- Log in and track the progress of your application.
- Visit the online UCAS bookshop of useful publications (with discounts for students).
- Link to Extra – to find an additional course to apply to, should you receive no offers.
- Get information about financing your studies.
- Go through Clearing – the placing system for those with no course offers.

Of course, applying through UCAS is no guarantee of a place on a higher education course. Every year, a number of individuals apply who do not get offered places. But this is the starting point of a whole new phase of your life, whether through a higher education course or an alternative learning route. Both pathways can lead to the personal fulfilment and independence that an interesting and worthwhile occupation or career can provide.

USING THIS GUIDE

This book is divided into three parts – a brief outline of the content and purpose of each one is given below.

PART I: IN THE THINK TANK
Before you make a UCAS application it is important that you thoroughly research all your higher education options. The first part of this guide gives you a number of ideas about those areas which need detailed consideration before you can be confident of making the right higher education course choices for *you*. Its six chapters guide you through the decision-making process, guiding students through the process of finding answers to key questions like:

- Is higher education the right option for me? (See Chapter 1)
- How will a degree fit in with my career plans? (see Chapter 2)

- How will I afford it? (See Chapter 3)
- How do I choose what and where to study? (See Chapters 4 and 5)
- Will I meet the entry requirements? (See Chapter 6)

You need to be ready to explain and justify your decision-making. Admissions tutors (who read your UCAS application and who may interview you) will want to know *why* you have applied for a place on their particular course!

At the end of each **In the think tank** chapter is a **Resources** section suggesting points of reference that can be accessed in your local careers library or Connexions centre. Ask advisers for help in finding the most up-to-date materials.

PART II: THE ADMISSIONS PROCEDURE – APPLICATIONS, INTERVIEWS, OFFERS AND BEYOND

Once you have decided which courses to apply for, the second part of the book gives you an overview of the entire admissions procedure. It works through the whole process, answering key questions like:

- When do I submit my application? (see Chapter 7)
- How do institutions communicate their offers to me? (See Chapter 7)
- How do I accept/decline offers? (See Chapter 7)
- What about non-standard applications? (See Chapter 8)
- How can I maximise my chances if I'm called for interview? (See Chapter 9)
- What happens on results day? (See Chapter 10)
- How do I use Clearing? (See Chapter 10)

PART III: USING APPLY TO SUBMIT YOUR UCAS APPLICATION

Part III of this book covers technicalities of filling in and submitting your UCAS application via Apply, taking you step-by-step through each area of the online form and offering helpful advice and tips on how to avoid the pitfalls. For the small number of applicants who – for whatever reason – are unable to apply online, details on completing a paper UCAS application are included in Appendix 1.

STAYING ON THE STRAIGHT AND NARROW – CALENDAR FOR ADVANCED-LEVEL STUDENTS

If you stick to the timetable, the whole process of applying to higher education is straightforward. The following calendar will give you an idea of what you should be doing and when – refer to the relevant chapters for further information.

	First year	
Autumn term	Start to explore the range of possible options to follow your advanced-level courses at school or college.	See Chapters 1 and 2
	Consider your GCSE or equivalent qualifications – the range and grades achieved – and review any AS/Scottish Higher or BTEC National modules that you are taking. Will your qualifications enable you to fulfil your future plans? Discuss this point with your careers/Connexions	See Chapter 6
Spring term	Work through a skills, aptitudes and interests guide, such as Centigrade or Morrisby, or complete a Career Development Profiling exercise.	See Chapter 2
	Start to research your higher education options in the light of these results. Prepare for and attend a UCAS higher education convention.	See Chapters 4 and 5
	Explore the financial implications of attending a higher education course.	See Chapter 3
Summer term	Prepare for and attend a UCAS convention – if missed out in spring.	See Chapters 4 and 5
	Continue to research your higher education options – checking UCAS course requirements and entry profiles. Draw up a shortlist of possible higher education institutions.	
	Attend at least two higher education open days or taster sessions.	
	Make decisions on courses/modules to take in your second year of advanced-level study.	Discuss with your school
	Arrange to do work experience during the summer. This is an important prerequisite for entry to some courses, eg paramedical studies, medicine, veterinary science/medicine, social sciences, the land-based industries and teaching degree courses.	See Chapter 2

Summer term	Try to enlist sponsorship for courses – write to possible organisations you have researched.	See Chapter 3
	Start to organise your year out if you plan to take a gap year.	
	Gather up material evidence from which to draft a Personal Statement for your UCAS application.	See Chapter 16
	Research financial support you may be entitled to and discuss the implications of your higher education choice with parents/guardians and advisers.	See Chapter 3
Second year		
Autumn term	Review your courses again – now that your summer exam results are known.	
	Before 20 September, consider whether to have your AS levels certificated. Get advice from your careers/ Connexions adviser or subject teacher, if unsure.	
	Between 1 September and 15 January – preferably as early as possible – submit your completed UCAS application using Apply.	See Chapter 7 and Part III
	Before 15 October, complete your UCAS application for Oxford or Cambridge. Oxford application cards and Cambridge's preliminary application forms should also be submitted before this date.	See Chapter 8 and Part III
	Before 15 October, submit all UCAS applications for entry to medicine, dentistry and veterinary science/ medicine.	
Spring term	**From 1 January**, Route B art and design applications will be processed. (UCAS accepts them from 1 September.)	
	By 15 January, all art and design course Route A applications need to be with UCAS. 15 January is the closing date for all standard applications from UK and EU students to be guaranteed equal academic consideration.	
	Apply for bursaries, sponsorship or scholarships – as appropriate.	See Chapter 3
	Prepare for possible interviews with admissions tutors; role play is useful here.	See Chapter 9
	7 March – applications to art and design courses through Route B need to be sent to UCAS by this advisory date (closing date is **24 March**).	See Chapter 8

Spring term	Applications for financial assessment should be returned to your local authority – whatever your particular circumstances.	
	From 26 February, if you used all five choices in your application, but are not holding an offer from a higher education institution, use the Extra option.	See Chapter 7
	By 31 March – higher education institutions are advised to send UCAS their decisions on all applications received by the 15 January deadline. (9 May is the absolute deadline for institutions to inform UCAS of their decisions.) Applicants are informed of decisions via Track, by post from UCAS and, often, by the higher education institution.	See Chapter 7
Summer term	**By 6 May**, decisions should have been received from all higher education institutions, and your responses made to any offers of higher education places which you hold.	See Chapter 7
	12 June is the last date for receiving art and design Route B applications before Clearing.	See Chapter 8
	Before the end of June, further applications can be made using Extra (if you applied for five courses originally and are not holding an offer). **30 June** is the last date for receipt of all applications before Clearing.	See Chapter 7
	21 August is A level results day, when you may need additional support through UCAS Clearing to find an alternative higher education option, or further information and guidance from your local careers or Connexions service. Vacancy information is available from this date.	See Chapter 10
	20 September is the last date for Clearing applications.	See Chapter 10

I

IN THE THINK TANK

1

IS HIGHER EDUCATION
RIGHT FOR YOU?

OVERVIEW OF HIGHER EDUCATION TODAY

In 2005, 285,110 18- to 19-year-olds started higher education courses in the
UK (source: Higher Education Statistics Agency), although the proportion of
mature students is on the rise. The main age range people applying to higher
education courses is therefore still 17 to 18. If you fall into this category,
application for entry to higher education may well be the most far-reaching
step that you've taken alone. There are plenty of individuals to consult to
help you choose your higher education course and place of study – for
example, your careers or Connexions adviser, careers and subject teachers,
present employer, parents*, wider family and friends. But the decision is
ultimately yours and, since it will affect your life for several years ahead, you
need to be confident about the suitability of your selected higher education
courses.

Every year, people take up places only to find that the course content,
teaching style or institution is not what they expected and, as a result, the
UK-wide drop-out rate from higher education is 15% (source: Higher
Education Funding Council for England). This is a waste of time, money and
resources – from the perspective both of students and of higher education
institutions – so it is worth taking the time at this stage to make sure that
your application choices are really appropriate for you.

*Throughout this book, the term parents *should be read to mean parents or legal guardians.*

ALL ABOUT YOU

Before considering higher education courses, there are a few points on which you really need to know your own mind – take a look at the questions posed in the following paragraphs and work out where you stand.

Are you happy to continue in education, full or part time, for a further two, three or four years?

Going on to higher education is a big step to take. Put simply, you've got to be committed and enthusiastic, and be expecting to enjoy the experience; if you're half-hearted and do not enjoy your studies, you will be wasting your time.

Advanced-level study (for example AS/A2 level, Scottish Higher, Irish Leaving Certificate, International Baccalaureate (IB), BTEC and so on) is essential preparative learning for many aspects of higher education, not just in terms of subject-specific knowledge, but also in terms of analytical skills. On your higher education course, you will be developing your powers of deduction, reasoning, critical analysis and evaluation just as much as you will be learning new facts about your chosen subject. Are you ready for this?

There are literally thousands of courses that are not straight developments of school- or college-based study – many are fascinating and worthwhile combinations that include opportunities for studying abroad. Does the thought of all this fill you with excitement or leave you pretty cold?

Do you have a strong and ongoing interest in self-development?

Your friends may already have started earning and could become 'independent adults' while you continue to study and accumulate sizeable debts. Can you be patient and philosophical, anticipating an interesting occupation and improved standard of living when you become an experienced graduate?

Do people around you (family, friends, girl-/boyfriend) appreciate and support your intention to continue your education? If they do not, do you anticipate that this will pose you practical or emotional challenges? And if they do, will they be as understanding (continuing to value and support your higher education endeavours) in two or three years' time?

Have you the mental strength to maintain self-belief, sticking to your long-term aims, should others withdraw their support? A willingness to discuss your intentions and consult with others may help everyone find ways to accept new realities.

Have you seriously explored your aptitudes, interests and career aspirations?

Do you want to learn more because you have strong ability in a particular skills area and because you find the subject matter interesting? If so, you are in a good starting position and are likely to enjoy your studies.

But some degree-level courses explore one particular subject area in great depth, with no obvious link to employment or a career structure (for example: history, anthropology, geography, physics, English, American studies or French). Have you thought about what you will do once you graduate? How will your degree link in with your longer-term career plan? (See **Chapter 2** for more on this.) A degree may only be a stepping stone to the start of many professional careers – once in employment, it is often necessary to continue studying to gain professional qualifications. You will need commitment!

Some people are influenced by promotional publicity or by the enthusiasm of others and do not consider the possible long-term impact of their choice on themselves. This point needs careful evaluation. Step back and try a number of aptitude and interest guides that are available online and in careers libraries and Connexions centres (see the Resources section at the end of **Chapter 2**). You need to investigate the values and attitudes underpinning your decision-making.

Are you ready to be a student?

Do not be surprised if you feel confused and uncertain about applying to courses at distant locations. You are taking an important decision which may result in you striking out on your own, seemingly leaving behind everything you are familiar with. It's natural to feel apprehensive about this – many people do experience insecurity and can feel isolated and disorientated at first, but most find they adapt very quickly.

If you are feeling very worried about the prospect of leaving home, work through these feelings with a friendly careers or Connexions adviser, student adviser or tutor and focus on positive aspects of your higher education intentions. A plan for self-development that includes degree-level study can be an indicator of a maturing individual.

Student life is likely to offer you all the social and extra-curricular opportunities you ever dreamed of – do you have confidence that you will be able to balance your social life with your studies? Remember, there is a big change from the guided learning you have experienced at school or college to the self-management of study in higher education. You will have to develop your own study skills and become an independent, self-motivated learner. Your subject teachers or tutors can offer helpful guidance on this point.

CONCLUSION

The decision to pursue a higher education course is not one that should be taken lightly. However, if you have read through the questions above and still feel confident that higher education is the right choice for you, read on. The rest of the **In the think tank** section of this book will help you focus your research so that you can cut down the seemingly infinite number of courses on offer to the five you will enter on your UCAS application.

As you work through the next six chapters, keep testing yourself by asking the following questions:

- Have I given enough consideration to this point?
- Which resources proved useful in my research?
- Have I talked to people with knowledge/experience in this area?
- Will I feel the same in two or three years' time?
- Should I do more investigating?

> **Tip**
>
> Firm decisions about your aims and intentions need to be taken by the end of September 2007 and all subsequent UCAS deadlines must be met. Make use of your local careers or Connexions service's *Options at 18+* booklet and pages 4–6 of this book to draw up your own calendar of important dates and deadlines.

2

LOOKING TO THE FUTURE

With such a lot of time and money committed to following a course of higher education, it is vital to have researched possible career routes leading on from university study. This is the moment for in-depth careers exploration and planning, looking at where a particular subject area might take you and also at where others have gone before.

Many people find the idea of life after education exciting and intimidating in equal measure. It can be difficult to face as it may seem that there is simply too much choice: how can you ever narrow down the options when you are having enough trouble even choosing which courses to apply for?

The important thing to remember is that any decisions you make or ideas you have at this stage are not set in stone. You can change and adapt your plans as you go along – but it's better to have a plan in the first place, not least because admissions tutors want to know that you are looking ahead, and that you are going to be an interested and engaged undergraduate with a career development plan that extends well beyond your time as a student. If you are called to interview (see **Chapter 9**), having thought things through thoroughly will mean you aren't floored by any career-related questions.

DEVELOPING A CAREER PLAN

IF YOU ALREADY HAVE A CAREER PLAN...
If you already have a particular career in mind, now is the time to research it in as much depth as possible, finding out which courses are the most

relevant, which get you professional accreditation and which have the best record of placing graduates in their chosen career area. For more on this, see **Chapters 4 and 5**.

IF YOU ALREADY KNOW WHAT SUBJECT INTERESTS YOU, BUT YOU DO NOT KNOW WHAT YOU WANT TO DO NEXT...

This is the time to do some broad research. Take a look at a careers directory or website (see **Resources** at the end of this chapter) to find out what's out there and focus in on the jobs that seem to relate to your chosen subject. Research possible progression routes and projected salaries in different careers.

You can also get ideas from the occupational destinations of graduates from major subject areas – this information is usually available on higher education institutions' websites. Find out how many of last year's completers were in 'graduate' occupations (drawing on their particular skills and abilities) six months after graduation.

IF YOU HAVE NO IDEA AT ALL...

If you're not sure what subject area interests you and you do not have a particular career in mind, it may be worth reconsidering whether higher education is likely to be a worthwhile way of spending your time or money. On the other hand, if you are simply feeling bewildered by the number of options available to you, there are plenty of books, websites and ICT programmes that can help you assess your interests. Try a range of them, and take it from there.

 Tip Remember that your careers/Connexions adviser is always a good starting point.

THE GRADUATE SKILL SET

Some courses lead naturally into a recognised career or occupational area (for example veterinary surgery, law or hospitality and catering management), but most do not. For the majority of students, therefore, the value of higher education in terms of career prospects is that it enables you to develop a 'graduate skills set', because study of *any* subject at higher education level should develop your abilities in the following areas:

- Logical, deductive reasoning
- Analytical research
- Creative problem-solving

- Cooperative teamwork and interpersonal skills (giving you the opportunity to take the lead on some projects)
- Clear presentation of ideas and projects
- Self-confidence
- Initiative, motivation and self-management
- Reliability, enthusiasm, flexibility and adaptability
- Key Skills (IT, Application of Number, Communication).

Having high level skills in all these areas will increase your appeal to prospective employers. However, most employers and some undergraduate courses will also require you to have demonstrated your interest in your chosen career area through work experience or work placements. This is a major reason why it's important to think hard about your career aspirations as early as possible.

Work experience

Many potential undergraduates have experience of the world of work but, for a number of courses (for example, those linked with health or social care and careers in the land-based industries), evidence of work experience in the field is an essential prerequisite for course entry.

If, as with around 41% of students, you have to work during term-time higher education (Unite *Student Experience Report 2007*), try to spend time in a job that will broaden your experience and give insight into a potential employment area. You can get help with finding suitable part-time and holiday work through your local careers or Connexions service and, when in higher education, from the university careers service's jobshop.

 Admissions tutors are impressed by those who have built up knowledge of a related work sector and whose plans include developing useful employment links while studying.

Conclusion

It's helpful to have a career path in mind, even if it's subject to review, change and adaptation as you progress through your course and gain experience. The earlier you start your research, the better your chance of making an informed decision – with the added benefit that evidence of your long-term approach will strengthen your UCAS application and improve your interview performance.

Resources

Publications:

- *Careers 2007* – overview of over 750 careers, useful as a starting point to get ideas (Trotman, www.trotman.co.uk)
- *If Only I'd Known* – tips on making the most of university and how to gain the skills that graduate employers are looking for (Association of Graduate Recruiters/Careers Services Unit/Association of Graduate Careers Advisory Services; available to download free on www.grb.uk.com)
- *Getting Into* series – gives advice on securing a place at university for courses leading to professional careers such as Medicine and Business & Management Courses (Trotman, www.trotman.co.uk)
- *Uncovered* series – in-depth look at graduate careers including Teaching, Law, Media, Accountancy and Marketing (Trotman, www.trotman.co.uk)
- *You Want to Do What?!* Volumes I and II – guide to some of the more unusual career options available (Trotman, www.trotman.co.uk)

ICT programs:

- Careerscape Multimedia – information on careers and higher education courses, together with case studies and articles (CASCAiD, www.cascaid.co.uk)
- Centigrade – gauges your academic and personal strengths (Cambridge Occupational Analysts, www.coa.co.uk)
- CID – Careers Information Database with information on over 920 occupations and links to relevant higher education courses (Careersoft, www.careersoft.co.uk)
- Job Explorer Database (JED) – interactive, multimedia careers information resource in which students can explore over 800 jobs in depth, with over 6000 pictures and 250 video case studies of people at work (Careersoft, www.careersoft.co.uk)
- KeyCLIPS – allows users to search for careers by factors such as work skills or school subjects, and also has a linked interest guide (Lifetime Careers Publishing, www.lcw.uk.com)

Websites:

- http://uk.tickle.com/career.html – personality profiling indicator test
- www.aimhigher.ac.uk – if you are considering whether higher education is right for you
- www.bbc.co.uk/radio1/onelife/work

- www.careersa-z.co.uk – alphabetical listing of careers with links to many other websites
- www.channel4.com/brilliantcareers – builds a profile of what you're like and what you like
- www.connexions-direct.com/jobs4u – careers database that can be searched via a combination of job families, interests, qualifications and working conditions
- www.learndirect-advice.co.uk – carries a databank of careers information, and also hosts a careers interest guide
- www.prospects.ac.uk – useful detailed information on graduate careers; the Prospects Planner area of the site sets questions to identify your abilities, skills and interests before defining the most important things that you want from work, linking these findings with specific careers
- www.trotman.co.uk – for a broad range of careers publications

3

A MATTER OF MONEY

There are two main costs of attending higher education:

- **Annual tuition fees** (top-up fees) range up to approximately £3070 for 2007–8, with most institutions opting to set them at the maximum level permitted by the government. (The exact figure for 2008–9 will be determined in spring 2008, but fees are pegged to rise only by the cost of living until 2010 and so should be about £3150.)
- **Living expenses** cover the cost of accommodation, food, clothes, travel and learning resources, as well as leisure and social activities.

How do you intend to fund your studies? Do not sidestep this issue! You'll need to deliberate carefully on how to finance your university studies over a number of years; your parents or partner and local authority education or student finance department should be involved in the discussion. This chapter gives a brief overview of what is a very complicated funding situation. Do look at the resources listed at the end of the chapter to get a more detailed understanding of how the system works.

FUNDING ARRANGEMENTS OVERVIEW

The exact funding situation varies depending on where you come from and where you plan to study.

RESIDENTS OF ENGLAND AND WALES

The cost of providing college and university courses is met partly by the government, but mainly by variable tuition fees – up to an annual maximum of around £3070 in 2007–8. You can choose to pay the fees up front or take out a **tuition fee loan**, which is not means tested. The Student Loans Company pays fees directly to the institution at the start of each year of the course, adding the cost to your repayable loan total.

Most universities also offer **tuition fee bursaries**, covering part or all of the cost. These are awarded on criteria of their choice, but they often use the level of your parental income or maintenance grant that you receive. Additional financial support is available to those with childcare costs or dependants, and to help students with disabilities.

You can apply for a **maintenance grant** (up to £2765 in 2007–8), for which you will be means tested. If you live in England or Wales and are financially dependent on your parents, then their single or joint income will be assessed by your local authority to gauge the level of maintenance grant you will be awarded. If you are independent, your financial assistance will be assessed on your likely earnings and financial responsibilities throughout the period of your studies.

You can also apply for a **maintenance loan**. In 2007–8, the maximum ranged from £3495 for non-London students living at home to £6315 for students living away from home in London. If you have not been means tested for a grant, you can borrow 100% of the maximum. However, if you have been means tested, even if you are eligible for no grant, you can only borrow 75% of the maximum. You should therefore work out in advance whether you are likely to get a grant. The Student Loans Company pays the maintenance loan directly into your bank account at the start of each term, if you have applied in advance.

> You are advised to apply to the appropriate authority for funding as soon as you have firmly accepted an offer of a place. You should not wait until a conditional offer is confirmed later in the year.

Both types of loan form a single account, which is not repayable until the April after graduation, and then you only pay 9% of your earnings over £15,000 per annum. There is interest accruing on this debt at a rate linked with inflation (about 3% at present). By the end of a three-year full-time course, you could owe the Student Loans Company £20–30,000, although with careful budget planning, a maintenance grant and a part-time job, you can keep this figure rather lower.

> Residents of England, Wales and Northern Ireland are advised to apply for assessment in order to establish their eligibility for assistance in future years, even if they expect to have to pay the full amount in their first year.

RESIDENTS OF SCOTLAND

Residents of Scotland do not have to pay tuition fees, regardless of where they study in the UK. However, all those who graduate will have to pay a 'higher education endowment' when their salary reaches a certain level. You may also be eligible for a non-repayable bursary as well as a part means-tested loan to help with living costs, for which you should apply to SAAS (Student Awards Agency for Scotland).

OVERSEAS STUDENTS

Students from EU countries may be eligible to have all or part of their tuition fees paid and, possibly, grant support to study at a UK higher education institution. They should apply to the appropriate authority for the institutions at which they firmly accept an offer, as follows:

- For institutions in England and Wales, you should apply to the Department for Education and Skills (DfES). The institutions at which you have firmly accepted an offer will be able to provide you with further details of whom to contact).
- For institutions in Scotland or Northern Ireland, you should contact SAAS (Student Awards Agency for Scotland) or the Northern Ireland Education and Library Board respectively.

Non-EU students from abroad receive no assistance.

OTHER SOURCES OF CASH

For many students, there will be a continual need to balance studies with **part-time employment**. A useful website with a great number of part-time jobs is www.hotrecruit.com. Another, with a particularly creative approach to the issue, is www.sliversoftime.com. However, many higher education courses include practical course work, field studies and/or time spent abroad, leaving little opportunity for employment except during vacations. Additionally, universities often recommend that students spend no more than 15 hours a week in paid employment, if their studies are not to suffer.

Many students take advantage of the student banking deals available from many of the high-street banks. These can include **interest-free overdrafts** as well as various other freebies such as free driving lessons or railcards. You should shop around carefully for the deal that best suits your priorities – and remember, the advice banks give on their websites is unlikely to be wholly impartial.

Tip	Try not to run up big bank overdrafts or especially credit card debts as, in the long run, you can end up paying large sums of interest on the money owed.

WILL YOU BE ELIGIBLE FOR EXTRA FINANCIAL HELP?

Students on particular courses, with particular career aspirations or with particular personal circumstances may be eligible for extra financial help. Here are a few examples:

- It is possible to get sponsorship from the Armed Forces and other employers/sectors of industry to help fund your studies.
- Some students win university or departmental scholarships and there are a number of university and college bursaries for different categories of applicant.
- There are NHS bursaries for students undertaking studies allied to medicine.
- Local authorities can access extra funds to help those with disabilities or who have dependants to care for.
- Disabled students may be eligible for a Disabled Students' Allowance or equivalent and for extra financial support and help with care.

There are several directories in which to research educational grants, and some that are particularly relevant for those in unusual or challenging circumstances. Every university has a student financial adviser whom individuals can approach for help. The Students' Union is also a good source of information and advice on financial assistance.

CONCLUSION

No student should be put off applying for a higher education course because of lack of financial help. That said, money can be a major headache for students so it is well worth taking the time to work out how you're going to fund yourself. It's also very important to be on top of all the paperwork required for loan applications, as missed deadlines can mean that you start your course before your loan comes through.

Resources

Publications:
- *The Educational Grants Directory 2006/07* (Directory of Social Change/Charities Aid Foundation, www.dsc.org.uk)
- *Everything You Wanted to Know about Sponsorship, Placements and Graduate Opportunities* (British Association for the Advancement of Science/Amoeba Publications, www.everythingyouwantedtoknow.com)

- *Students' Money Matters 2007* (Trotman, www.trotman.co.uk)
- *Student Support and Benefits Handbook: England Wales and Northern Ireland 2007/08* and *Benefits for Students in Scotland Handbook 2007/08* (Child Poverty Action Group, www.cpag.org.uk)
- *University Scholarships, Awards & Bursaries* (Trotman, www.trotman.co.uk)

Websites (official bodies):
- www.dfes.gov.uk/studentsupport – the DfES site with detailed information for every higher education applicant, plus contact details for your local authority in England
- http://bursarymap.direct.gov.uk – interactive map linking to the bursary pages of all higher education institutions
- www.studentfinancewales.co.uk – Wales
- www.student-support-saas.gov.uk – Scotland
- www.delni.gov.uk – Northern Ireland
- www.slc.co.uk – the Student Loans Company

Websites (general student support):
- www.connexions.gov.uk
- www.everythingyouwantedtoknow.com
- www.funderfinder.org.uk
- www.fundingforlearners.co.uk
- www.nhscareers.nhs.uk
- www.nusonline.co.uk – the National Students' Union site
- www.studentsupportdirect.co.uk
- www.studentzone.org.uk/finance – useful for EU and overseas students
- www.support4learning.org.uk
- www.ucas.com/studentfinance

Websites (jobs):
- www.hotrecruit.com
- www.sliversoftime.com

4

CHOOSING WHAT TO STUDY

You are entitled to enter five* course choices on your UCAS application. You are probably already aware that a vast number of subjects are on offer – you can get an idea of the full range by exploring the UCAS website course search facility and the other resources listed on pages 16 and 31. So how do you start to narrow it down? This chapter covers some of the questions you should be asking yourself, so that you can focus your research on the courses that will be best suited to your interests.

WHICH SUBJECT AREA?

If you have got this far, then it is likely that you have some idea of what subject area you would like to pursue further. If not, however, here are a few questions to think about:

- Which of your advanced-level subjects interests you most? Are you interested enough to want to study it for another three years?
- Are you interested in one particular aspect of your advanced-level course? If so, you may find that specialist higher education courses will allow you to focus on this particular aspect.
- What are your career aspirations? What are the entry requirements for that career? Which courses match up best?
- Are you prepared to undergo more specific job-related training as a postgraduate? If not, then should you be looking for a vocational course that leads directly into an occupation?

*Applicants are limited to four medicine, dentistry or veterinary science course choices but can make one additional application to a course in another subject – see Chapter 8 for more information.

Try an exercise to determine which subjects you are interested in, such as the Stamford Test on the UCAS website, or use a predictor like Centigrade to indicate courses that might appeal to you (the **Resources** section at the end of **Chapter 2** should give you some more ideas). Also, try the student exercises in the book *Getting In Getting On*.

WHICH QUALIFICATION?

It is important to know something about each of the different types of qualifications on offer so that you can select the one that is most suitable for you. For example, course length (and consequent expense) varies widely. A list of the main options is given below; then each course type is explored in more depth in the paragraphs that follow:

- Diplomas of Higher Education
- Higher National Diplomas
- Foundation degrees
- Ordinary or honours first degrees
- Courses leading to the award of a master's degree.

DIPLOMAS OF HIGHER EDUCATION (DIPHES)
Some universities and colleges offer undergraduate diplomas (defined as full-time or sandwich two- or three-year DipHE courses). Your policy with regard to application should be the same as for HNDs (see below).

HIGHER NATIONAL DIPLOMAS (HNDS)
Many universities and colleges offer BTEC or SQA HND courses lasting two years. These are often offered in the same subject areas as the university's degree courses, giving students the option to transfer between courses and top up their HND to a degree through a further year's study. Keep this in mind when planning your application strategy. With a few exceptions, HNDs fall into two main subject areas: science and engineering, or business studies and related subjects. Your approach to these areas should be quite different...

SCIENCE AND ENGINEERING
Science and engineering courses at all levels attract comparatively fewer applications than business and finance courses. It is therefore likely that, if you apply for a degree in, for example, mechanical engineering at an institution which also offers an HND in engineering, admissions tutors will make you an offer covering both the degree and the HND course, but with different conditions for each (normally lower for the HND).

If you can achieve the minimum entry qualifications for a degree course, you should aim for these grades in subject areas such as science and engineering, *unless* you positively want to take a more vocational HND course (which many students do).

BUSINESS STUDIES AND RELATED SUBJECTS

For HND courses in this subject area the picture is rather different. HND courses usually attract a large number of applications in their own right: many students deliberately opt for the HND courses because they are shorter and often more specialised than their degree counterparts. It is therefore very unusual for institutions to make dual offers for degrees and HNDs. This means that you must consider your options very carefully. If you have doubts about your ability to reach the level required for degree entry, you may be best advised to apply for the HND.

 Tip You *must* talk through the options with your school, college or careers adviser before making these difficult decisions.

OTHER SUBJECTS

Of course, there are some very specialised subject areas where the number of courses available is limited and you may *only* have the option of the HND – examples include management of textile aftercare, minerals resource management or leather technology.

FOUNDATION DEGREES

Most universities, in partnership with higher and further education colleges, offer foundation degrees. These usually last two years and, like HNDs, can be converted into honours degrees with a subsequent year of full-time study.

Designed by business and industry to meet their new skills needs, foundation degrees were originally developed to train employees in particular career sectors as higher technicians or associate professionals. Admissions tutors initially looked for appropriate commercial or technical experience rather than academic qualifications. However, many students are now accepted for foundation degree study who intend to work in a particular sector but have, as yet, little or no experience.

Foundation degrees combine academic study with the development of work-related skills. There are over a thousand full-time, part-time and distance learning options in areas such as digital media arts, business and management, horticulture, equine studies, hospitality, fashion design and a vast range of other subjects.

In 2006, 14,691 applications were made to foundation degrees – a 17.4% rise on the previous year. All potential full-time foundation degree students use Apply for entry to courses; part-time applicants make a direct application to individual colleges. There is further information about foundation degrees on www.ucas.com and www.fdf.ac.uk.

DEGREE COURSES

BACHELOR'S DEGREES

First degree courses usually last three years (sometimes four, if a year abroad or in industry is included) and lead to the award of a bachelor's degree. The title of the degree awarded usually reflects the subject studied; some of the more common ones are listed below:

- BA   Bachelor of Arts
- BSc   Bachelor of Science
- LLB   Bachelor of Law
- BMus   Bachelor of Music
- BCom   Bachelor of Commerce
- BEng   Bachelor of Engineering.

The exceptions to this are Oxford and Cambridge Universities, which award a BA regardless of the subject. (Oxbridge graduates are then able to upgrade to a master's degree without further exams, about four years later.)

MASTER'S DEGREES

In England and Wales, master's degrees are usually acquired via a completely different course which must be applied for separately and cannot be taken until the bachelor's degree has been completed. However, some first-degree courses lead directly to the award of a master's degree (eg MEng, MSci, MPhys or MEd). These courses are usually extended or enhanced versions of the bachelor's course, lasting at least four years, and are likely to be in Engineering or Science disciplines.

In some Scottish universities, the first degree is a master's (MA) degree which takes four years. Most students enter university or college in Scotland at 18 after six years of secondary education. (A significant minority, however, enter after only five years.)

SINGLE, JOINT OR COMBINED HONOURS?

Most higher education institutions offer single, joint and combined honours courses – the latter of which enable you to combine several areas of interest and may lead you to an interesting perspective or additional career opportunities (for example, studying Biology with French may enable you to work in France).

However, if you intend to take a joint or combined honours course, do be aware that you will be kept busier than on a single honours course. It can be a struggle if you have to make your own connections between the modules of study and the work may not be well-coordinated. Ask individual department admissions tutors questions early about combining courses.

DEGREE CLASSIFICATION

Honours degrees are classified as:

- First class
- Second class – upper division (2:1)
- Second class – lower division (2:2)
- Third class.

Ordinary and pass degrees are awarded, depending on the system, to those not pursuing honours courses, or to narrow failures on honours courses.

WHICH MODE OF STUDY?

Many degrees and HNDs can be studied as sandwich courses – these come in two varieties:

- **Thick sandwich courses** – these include a full year spent on an industrial, commercial or professional training placement.
- **Thin sandwich courses** – these include several sessions of a few weeks' work experience spread throughout the course.

Sponsorship is sometimes tied in with sandwich courses. Normally, you apply for a sandwich degree/HND course through UCAS and your higher education institution arranges your training placement. However, if a sponsor requires you to attend a particular university or college, the sponsor will inform you and the higher education institution will sort out the UCAS arrangements.

You may also be able to choose between **full-time** and **part-time** courses – the latter is becoming more popular as students increasingly find it necessary to work to finance their studies; on the other hand, it can be difficult to balance the demands of a job and higher education, so you should make sure you do some thorough research.

WHICH COURSES?

The million-dollar question! Having thought about the above points, you should now have a clearer idea of the type of qualification and subject area you would like to apply for. However, there may still be hundreds of courses on offer fitting the criteria you have laid down so far – so this is the point where you must really start to narrow down your options. The only way to do this is by thorough research – which means looking through directories, prospectuses and websites.

Here are some of the things you should take into account:

- **Course content** – there can be a whole world of difference between courses with exactly the same title, so take a detailed look at the content and see how it relates to your particular interests. How much do you want to specialise? How much freedom do you want to select your options?
- **Teaching and assessment methods** – again, these can vary widely. For example, some courses may be very practical, with workshops and case studies, and others may be centred round essays and tutorials. If you do not perform well in exams, you can search for courses assessed via modules and projects.
- **Professional accreditation** – if you are planning to enter a specific career for which professional accreditation is required (for example, Law, Engineering or Accountancy) then it is well worth checking out which courses offer full or partial exemption from the exams required to gain this accreditation.
- **Links with industry** – some courses and departments will maintain strong links with industry, which can help graduates secure jobs.
- **Graduate destinations** – these are often available on institutions' websites and can help you assess whether the course gives you the skills you will need in the workplace.

CONCLUSION

Based on these factors, you should be able to begin to develop a clear idea of the kind of course you would like to apply for. However, two aspects of the decision-making process have yet to be discussed – entry requirements and your choice of institution. These factors are examined in detail in the following chapters.

Resources

Publications:
- *Big Guide 2008 entry* (UCAS, www.ucasbooks.com)
- *CRAC Degree Course Guides* (Trotman, www.trotman.co.uk)
- *Which Degree? 2007*, 2 volumes (Trotman, www.trotman.co.uk)
- *Degree Course Offers 2008 entry* – will inform you whether, realistically, you are likely to meet course entry criteria (Trotman, www.trotman.co.uk)
- *Getting In Getting On 2008* (UCAS, www.ucasbooks.com)
- *Open Days 2007* (UCAS, www.ucasbooks.com)
- *Progression to... 2007 entry* series (UCAS, www.ucasbooks.co.uk)
- *Sixthformer's Guide 2007* (ISCO, www.isco.org.uk)
- *Trotman's Green Guides 2008* – Art, Design and Performing Arts; Healthcare; Physical Sciences (Trotman, www.trotman.co.uk)
- *What Do Graduates Do? 2007* – (Graduate Prospects)
- *You Want to Study What?!* Volumes I and II (Trotman, www.trotman.co.uk)

ICT programs:
- Higher Ideas – generates suggested higher education courses based on current studies, interests and career ambitions (Careersoft, www.careersoft.co.uk)

Websites:
- www.ucas.com – UCAS course search facility and Apply
- www.aimhigher.ac.uk – download the *Thinking it Through* booklet
- www.coursediscover.co.uk
- www.qaa.ac.uk
- www.uni4me.com

5

CHOOSING WHERE TO STUDY

The previous chapter should have helped you build up a picture of your ideal course, and start to create a shortlist. However, it's still likely that a lot more than five courses will fit the bill – so you need to narrow the list down further. Now is the time to start thinking about which institution you would like to study at.

WORKING OUT WHAT YOUR PRIORITIES ARE

You can apply through UCAS to over 300 higher education institutions across the UK, and very different considerations and priorities affect each applicant's choice of institution. To give you some idea of the range, present-day undergraduates say they were influenced by one or more of the following factors:

- Location (Do you prefer an urban or a rural setting? Do you want to be on a campus or in the middle of a city? Are you trying to stay in easy reach of home, or get as far away as possible?)
- Size of university
- Popularity of university
- Facilities for sport, leisure activities, music etc
- Accommodation (Is there enough of it? Does it suit your preferences – eg self-catering or with meals provided?)
- Famous alumni
- Good price of beer
- Male to female ratio(!).

On a more serious note, they also mention these influences:

- Reputation for research or particular specialism within a particular department
- Quality of course teaching
- Status of university as a whole (this can be a perplexing concept – if you feel concerned on this point, you will need to seek advice from professional bodies and/or large employers)
- Employability of a particular institution's graduates
- Number of student places on particular courses (the bigger the intake target, usually the better your chances – prospectuses give an indication of the size of intake, but remember that the numbers may include students on both single and combined or modular degrees)
- Entry requirements (be honest with yourself about your prospects at advanced level – it is better to face reality now than to be forced to revise your plans several months later)
- Cost of living
- Financial support offered to students (eg via bursaries and scholarships)
- Level of support and facilities for students with disabilities.

The list of factors you might want to consider could go on forever… you will have to draw the line somewhere and then work out which ones are most important to you personally. But even once you have decided on your key priorities, where do you start to find out the answers to all your questions? The **Resources** section at the end of this chapter lists publications where this type of information is brought together – referring to these as a first port-of-call can speed up your research no end, but there is no substitute for first-hand research (via university open days, websites and prospectuses). It is also well worth talking to former school leavers, family friends and older siblings about their experiences. More advice on this is given in the **Researching your shortlist** section, below.

 Do not forget to pick up university prospectuses and look at their websites.

STAYING CLOSE TO HOME?

A growing number of students only apply to higher education institutions that are within daily commuting distance, opting to save on living expenses while enjoying the support and comforts of home. With annual living expenses topping £5000 and variable tuition fees of up to £3070 per annum (2007 entry), the choice of living in halls of residence or in rented accommodation within a university town may be an option for fewer and fewer students.

On the other hand, studying from home can limit your 'student experience' as time spent travelling cuts down your opportunities for involvement in higher education societies. You may also be less likely to network and make new friends, especially if you still have close friends from school living in the area. For parents and siblings, having a full-time student living at home can create tensions as time goes by.

You may decide on a part solution: a growing number of higher education courses – HNDs, foundation degrees, even first degree courses – start with a year studying at a local, franchised further education college, before you transfer to the parent campus to complete your degree.

RESEARCHING YOUR SHORTLIST

As soon as you feel ready, draw up your shortlist of about ten possible courses from which you will select up to five (or four) final choices for your UCAS application. For each of your shortlist entries, make sure you have considered the following:

- What will I actually be studying on this course?
- Do I like the environment and where will I live?
- Will I be able to select any options on this course?
- How is progress assessed?
- Is there a tutorial system and how much support and advice on learning do students get?
- Can I achieve the qualifications needed for entry? (For help on this last point, see the next chapter.)

Attend open days and taster sessions at higher education institutions that really appeal, and talk with student ambassadors who will attempt to answer your questions on any subject. You can find information on these in the UCAS booklet *Open Days 2007*. You can also write and arrange a visit to the department by yourself. Make sure you have also spent time in the town or city where the institution is based; it is really important that you have experience of a place where you may spend three or four years.

For students with disabilities, this is particularly important – you need to make sure *before you apply* to an institution that it will be able to meet your particular needs. For example, some campuses are better than others for wheelchairs, while some have special facilities for the visually impaired or the deaf. Get in touch with the Disability Officers at your shortlisted universities or colleges – you can find their contact details on the Skill website (see the **Resources** section at the end of the chapter). More information about access and facilities for students with disabilities is also available on www.ucas.com and, of course, from the prospectuses and websites of higher education institutions.

Parents can help with weighing up the issues and are excellent as sounding boards, but their advice and knowledge on today's degree courses, their applicability and relevance, may well be out of date. (For example, some of the new UK universities have the best resourced and most reputable courses of applied study which feed into new careers in multimedia and technological industries – but equally, some of the newer institutions are under-resourced and have poor teaching reputations.)

 Tip If you feel at all unsure about your choice of subject, enquire at each of your shortlisted institutions to find out whether it is possible to transfer from one course to another once your studies have started.

Do not take anything as given. Phone departments directly and ask to speak to the admissions tutor if you want to ask questions about the destinations of course graduates, possible career progression, admission details – anything! Tutors can be helpful and informative; they aren't just there to teach. Many higher education institutions also supply 'Entry Profiles' for their courses – accessible on the UCAS website – which can help with the decision-making process. You should also attend your nearest UCAS higher education convention to talk directly with university tutors about courses.

Read the detail concerning courses that interest you and where you think, realistically, that you can match the entry requirements. Highlight important points you may want to address in the personal statement in your UCAS application, or refer to at interview, several months ahead.

 Tip Keep the prospectuses of places that you are definitely applying to!

SELECTING THE FINAL FIVE

If there is one particular university or college you want to attend (perhaps because you are a mature student and cannot move away from home) then you can use your choices to apply for more than one course at the same institution. (This is not possible at Oxbridge.) On the other hand, at some universities or colleges it is not necessary to apply for more than one course because admission is to a faculty or group of related subjects.

The other major factor to consider in selecting your final five courses is the entry requirements – in order to maximise your chance of success you need to make sure you apply to courses which are likely to make you an offer corresponding roughly with the grades you expect to achieve. This issue is examined in greater detail in the next chapter.

Resources

Publications:
- *Choosing Your Degree Course and University* (Trotman, www.trotman.co.uk)
- *Open Days 2007* (UCAS, www.ucasbooks.com)
- *Disabled Students' Guide to University* (Trotman, www.trotman.co.uk)
- *Student Book 2008* (Trotman Publishing, www.trotman.co.uk)
- *The Times Good University Guide 2007* (BooksFirst/HarperCollins, www.booksfirst.co.uk)
- *The Ultimate University Ranking Guide* (Trotman, www.trotman.co.uk)
- *The Virgin 2008 Alternative Guide to British Universities* (Virgin Books, www.virginbooks.com)
- *You Want to Study Where?!* (Trotman, www.trotman.co.uk)

Websites (for students with disabilities):
- www.rnib.org.uk – Royal National Institute for the Blind
- www.rnid.org.uk – Royal National Institute for the Deaf
- www.skill.org.uk – Skill: National Bureau for Students with Disabilities, Chapter House, 18–20 Crucifix Lane, London SE1 3JW; Tel: 0800 328 5050; Minicom: 0800 328 5050
- www.direct.gov.uk/en/disabledpeople

Websites (general):
- www.hero.ac.uk/uk/universities___colleges (three underscores) – has a comprehensive UK map showing the locations, and linking through to the websites, of higher education institutions
- www.push.co.uk – has a powerful search feature that can suggest the right university for you
- www.qaa.ac.uk/reviews – reports on the quality of teaching at individual higher education institution departments
- www.ucas.com/getting/events – details on spring and summer UCAS educational conventions
- www.ucas.com/instit – institution guides

6

ACADEMIC REQUIREMENTS

You may have been thinking about whether you will be able to fulfil higher education entry requirements since Year 10 or 11, carefully planning how your AS and A levels, Scottish Highers, IB, ILC or BTEC National modules will build a sound educational background from which to move on to higher education. On the other hand, you may not yet have given the matter any serious thought.

It is important to make sure you are realistic about the grades you hope to achieve and that you target your applications accordingly. This chapter will help you understand how institutions express their entry requirements and offer some basic dos and don'ts relating to the final five courses you select.

WHAT MIGHT THE ENTRY REQUIREMENTS BE?

Would-be higher education entrants normally need to achieve minimum qualifications equivalent to one of the following options:

- 2 A levels or Advanced Highers
- 1 12-unit Applied A level
- 1 BTEC National
- 1 NVQ at level 3.

You will also need supporting GCSEs/S grades at grades A*–C/1–3. (Requirements vary for mature students and other groups – see page 41.) In reality, however, most institutions require more than the basic minimum and many demand particular subjects for entry – there are two main reasons for this:

1 | Coping with the course: For study of some subjects, a higher education department or faculty can decide that all its students need to achieve a particular qualification (say, B or C in A level Maths) in order to cope with the course.
2 | Rationing places: Where there is high demand for a course, the entry requirements will rise, because if a department asks for three Bs, fewer applicants will qualify for entry than if three Cs are requested (even though the three-C candidates might cope perfectly well with the course). So grade requirements are used as a way of rationing places.

The latter of these two reasons is the more common – and it's therefore worth being aware that high grades are often an indication of *popularity*, not always of quality. Some universities, colleges and courses are more popular than others and can therefore set high grades if they feel that the 'market' in a particular subject will bear them – for example:

- Oxford and Cambridge Universities can ask for particularly high levels of performance.
- Particularly popular courses for 2007 entry included: pre-clinical medicine, law, social work, nursing, sports science, management science, design studies, computer science, psychology, accountancy, history and English. Indeed any course with a special feature (such as sponsorship or an exchange with an institution overseas) can attract large numbers of applications and may therefore require high grades.

Whatever the course you apply for, your qualifications are bound to be examined carefully by admissions tutors. They will be looking at your advanced-level study and checking that you are:

- Offering the right subjects to satisfy entry requirements.
- Offering subjects they are prepared to include in an offer.
- Offering the *types* of qualifications they want (eg AS and A levels, BTEC National).
- Offering the right number of qualifications.
- Making an effort to fill any gaps in your record (eg by retaking GCSE maths alongside your A levels).

Admissions tutors will be on the lookout for students who are repeating A levels; your UCAS application must give full details of your results at the first attempt and include details of what you are repeating and when (see **Chapter 15**). (Further explanations should be saved for your personal statement.)

Many will also attach a lot of importance to your results at GCSE or Scottish Standard level. After all, they will usually be the only evidence of your academic achievement to date. Admissions tutors will be looking for:

- A reasonable spread of academic qualifications
- Key subjects (eg English language and maths – even if the university or college does not require them, most employers do)
- A sound basis for sixth-form (or equivalent advanced-level) study
- Signs of academic capacity or potential.

ADDITIONAL AND ALTERNATIVE ENTRY REQUIREMENTS

Applicants to music, art and design and other **creative or performing arts courses** often have to compile a portfolio of work in an appropriate format, and may also have to attend an audition.

Should you wish to train for **work with young children or vulnerable adults** (for example in teaching, social work or the healthcare professions), the university or college will ask you to agree to have a criminal record check and you may also need an *enhanced disclosure document* – see **Chapter 12** for further details.

Applicants for **healthcare courses** such as medicine, dentistry, nursing or midwifery are advised to be immunised against Hepatitis B and may be asked to supply certificates to show they are not infected with it. You should check the immunisation requirements with the institutions you have chosen.

If you intend to apply for **vocational courses** then work experience may be an essential prerequisite for entry. You should check this well before applying to give you time to acquire it if necessary.

Students with certain disabilities may also be offered different entry requirements – it is worth checking with admissions tutors of individual courses as the criteria for admission may be relaxed.

MATURE STUDENTS
There is no single definition of a 'mature' applicant, but most higher education institutions now classify students as mature if they are over 21 years of age (20 in Scotland) at the date of entry to a course. The vast majority of departments welcome applications from mature students, and many (especially in science) would like more.

As a mature student, you are more likely to be accepted with qualifications that are unorthodox or would simply not be enough if they were presented by a student aged 18 in full-time education. That said, there is still fierce competition for places, and in most subjects places are not set aside for mature students. If you are favourably considered, you are likely to be called for interview.

It is not usually advisable to rely only on qualifications gained several years ago at school; university and college departments will want to see recent evidence of your academic ability so that they can evaluate your application fairly. In addition, taking a course of study at the right level helps prepare you for full-time student life.

Entry requirements for mature students are difficult to quantify because of these reasons – but a good approach might be to go to a further education college and study for one of the usual post-16 qualifications (eg A level or BTEC) or take one of the **Access to Higher Education** or **Foundation** courses specially designed for mature students. You may also find that you can get **Accreditation of Prior Learning (APL)** to recognise the skills you have developed in the workplace – see the UCAS website in the **Resources** section at the end of the chapter for more information.

It is extremely important for mature students to contact departments directly to ask about their admissions policies *before applying to UCAS*, and to tailor their applications accordingly.

HOW ARE ENTRY REQUIREMENTS EXPRESSED?

Entry requirements may be expressed as specific grades (eg BBC at A level or ABBB at Scottish Higher), as a target number of UCAS tariff points (eg 280 points) or as a mixture of the two (eg 280 points, including at least grade B in A level Chemistry).

THE UCAS TARIFF

The UCAS tariff system is a facility to assist higher education institutions in expressing entrance requirements and making conditional offers. It is not obligatory for higher education institutions to use the tariff (although they are encouraged to do so – and, for 2008 entry, over 76% of institutions expressed entry requirements using the tariff). The UCAS tariff:

■ Is a points system to report achievement for entry to higher education.
■ Gives numerical values to qualifications.
■ Establishes agreed equivalences between different types of qualifications.

- Allows comparison between applicants with different types of achievement.

For each qualification covered by the tariff, points are awarded for each different grade available. At present, the qualifications covered by the tariff are:

- GCE Double Awards, GCE A levels, GCE AS Double Awards and GCE AS levels
- Scottish Highers and Advanced Highers
- Scottish Standard Grades and Intermediate 2 awards
- Welsh Baccalaureate Advanced Diploma
- Irish Leaving Certificate
- International Baccalaureate
- BTEC National Awards, Certificates and Diplomas
- OCR National Certificates, Diplomas and Extended Diplomas
- Advanced Extension Awards (AEAs)
- Advanced Placement Programme
- Freestanding Mathematics qualifications at Level 3
- Diploma in Foundation Studies (Art and Design)
- The Key Skills of Application of Number, Communication and IT at Levels 2, 3 and 4
- The three wider Key Skills of Improving Own Learning and Performance, Problem Solving and Working with Others
- Scottish Core Skills of Communication, Numeracy, IT, Problem Solving and Working with Others
- Music examinations at grades 6–8
- Speech and Drama examinations at grades 6–8
- CACHE Diploma in Childcare and Education
- Institute of Financial Services (IFS) Certificate in Financial Studies (CeFS) and Diploma in Financial Studies (DipFS)
- British Horse Society Stage 3 Horse Knowledge & Care, Stage 3 Riding and Preliminary Teacher's Certificate
- Diploma in Fashion Retail
- iPRO Certificate and Diploma
- Certificate of Personal Effectiveness (COPE).

This year is the sixth time that admissions tutors will be dealing with the newer qualifications (eg Applied A levels, GCE AS levels) and the UCAS points tariff and, while they should be used to it now, you should check with individual universities and colleges to see what their policy is with regard to the newer qualifications included in the UCAS points tariff, such as Key Skills. Although all institutions are encouraged to use the tariff, not all incorporate it fully into their offers system, and you want to be sure that you will be considered on the basis of your qualifications.

CALCULATING YOUR TARIFF TOTAL

Here are a few general rules to help you calculate your tariff total:

- Points can be aggregated from different qualifications (eg GCE A level/AS level), although bear in mind that once an AS level has been certificated it cannot count towards the full A level.
- There is no double counting – students cannot count the same or similar qualifications twice (see www.ucas.com and exam boards' guidelines for more information on this).
- AS level points are subsumed into A level points in the same subject.
- Scottish Higher points are subsumed into Advanced Higher points in the same subject.
- Scottish Core Skills points at Intermediate 2 are subsumed into the points for Higher Core Skills.
- Key Skills achievement at a lower level (level 1 or 2) is subsumed into the highest level of achievement in that skill, eg level 2, 3 or 4, according to the circumstances.
- Many higher education courses accept Key Skills points scores in part-fulfilment of points offers.
- All certificated Key Skills achievement in Application of Number, Communication and IT, whether achieved through proxy qualifications or not, will attract the points indicated on the chart and proxies will not be regarded as double counting.
- There is no ceiling to the number of points that can be accumulated. This means that the tariff can recognise the full breadth and depth of students' achievements.

Do be aware that, **where institutions provide an entry requirement or a conditional offer as a points score, they will often make more specific demands about how those points are made up** in order to ensure that students starting their course have a certain depth of understanding in relevant subjects. For example, they may specify two A level passes at a certain grade in specified subjects, or exclude certain qualifications from being used to count in fulfilment of the requirement.

The current version of the UCAS tariff points table is shown on pages 45–7, and further guidance is available on the UCAS website.

TABLE OF UCAS TARIFF POINTS

GCE AS/AS VCE	GCE AS Double Award	GCE A level/AVCE	GCE/AVCE Double Award	BTEC Award	BTEC Certificate	BTEC Diploma	OCR Certificate	OCR Diploma	OCR Extended Diploma	Points	Irish Higher	Irish Ordinary	Scottish Advanced Higher	Scottish Higher	Scottish Int 2	Scottish Standard Grade	AP Group A	AP Group B
						DDD			D1	360								
						DDM			D2/M1	320								
						DMM			M2	280								
			AA		DD	MMM		D	M3	240								
			AB							220								
			BB		DM	MMP		M1	P1	200								
			BC		MM	MPP				180								
			CC		MP	PPP		M2/P1	P2	160								
			CD							140								
	AA	A	DD	D	PP		D	P2	P3	120			A				5	5
	AB									110								
	BB	B	DE							100			B				4	4
	BC									90	A1							
	CC	C	EE	M				P3		80			C					
										77	A2							
										72			D	A				
										71	B1							
	CD									70								
										64	B2							
A	DD	D		P						60				B			3	3
										58	B3							
										52	C1							
B	DE									50								
										48				C				
										45	C2							
							P			42				D				
C	EE	E								40					A			
										39	C3	A1						
										38						Band 1		
										35					B			
										33	D1							
D										30					C			
										28						Band 2		
										26	D2	A2						
E										20	D3	B1						
										14		B2						
										7		B3						

[1] The points shown are for the newly specified BTEC National Award, Certificate and Diploma introduced into centres from September 2002

[2] Further information on OCR grades and Tariff points can be found on the UCAS website

[3] The points shown for the Advanced Placement Programme come into effect for entry to higher education in 2008 onwards. Details of the subjects covered by each group can be found on the UCAS website

| BTEC Nationals in Early Years | | | CACHE Diploma in Child Care & Education | | Points | Diploma in Foundation Studies (Art and Design) | Diploma in Fashion Retail[4] | iPRO[5] | | AAT NVQ Level 3 in Accounting[6] |
Theory Diploma	Theory Certificate	Practical	Theory	Practical				Certificate	Diploma	
DDD					320					
					285	D				
DDM					280					
DMM					240					
			AA		225	M				
MMM					220					
	DD				200					
MMP			BB		165	P				
	DM	D			160		D			P
MPP	MM		CC	A	120		M			
		M	DD	B	100		P		Pass	
PPP	MP			C	80			Pass		
		P	EE	D	60					
	PP			E	40					

[4] The points for ABC's Diploma in Fashion Retail come into effect for entry to higher education in 2008 onwards
[5] The points for OCR's iPRO Certificate and Diploma come into effect for entry to higher education in 2008 onwards
[6] Points for the AAT Level 3 NVQ in Accounting come into effect for entry to higher education in 2009 onwards

| British Horse Society[7] | | | Points | Music Examinations[8] | | | | | | Speech & Drama Examinations[9] | | | |
| Stage 3 Horse Knowledge & Care | Stage 3 Riding | Preliminary Teacher's Certificate | | Practical | | | Theory | | | | | | |
				Grade 6	Grade 7	Grade 8	Grade 6	Grade 7	Grade 8	Grade 6	Grade 7	Grade 8	PCertLAM[10]
			90										
			80										D
			75			D						D	M
			70			M						M	
			65										P
			60		D						D		
			55		M	P					M	P	
			50										
			45	D						D			
			40	M	P					M	P		
Pass		Pass	35										
	Pass		30						D				
			25	P				D	M	P			
			20					M	P				
			15					P					
			10										
			5										

[7] The points for the British Horse Society (BHS) Awards come into effect for entry to higher education in 2008 onwards
[8] Points shown are for ABRSM, Guildhall, LCMM, Rockschool and Trinity College London advanced level music examinations
[9] Points shown are for LAMDA, LCMM and Trinity Guildhall advanced level speech and drama examinations accredited by the National Qualifications Framework and come into effect for entry to higher education in 2008 onwards. A full list of the subjects covered can be found on the UCAS website.
[10] Points for the LAMDA Level 3 Certificate in Speech and Drama: Performance Studies (PCertLAM) come into effect for entry to higher education in 2009 onwards

International Baccalaureate[11] Diploma	Points
45	768
44	744
43	722
42	698
41	675
40	652
39	628
38	605
37	582
36	559
35	535
34	512
33	489
32	466
31	442
30	419
29	396
28	373
27	350
26	326
25	303
24	280

[11] The points for the International Baccalaureate (IB) come into effect for entry to higher education in 2008 onwards and are awarded to candidates who achieve the IB Diploma

Free standing Maths[12]	IFS CeFS[13]	IFS DipFS[14]	COPE[15]	Advanced Extension Awards[16]	Points	Core Skills	Key Skills	Welsh Baccalaureate Core[17]
					120			Pass
			Pass		70			
		A			60			
		B			50			
		C		D	40			
		D			30		Level 4	
A	A	E		M	20	Higher	Level 3	
B	B				17			
C	C				13			
D	D				10	Int 2	Level 2	
E	E				7			

[12] Covers free-standing Mathematics qualifications – Additional Maths, Using and Applying Statistics, Working with Algebraic and Graphical Techniques, Modelling with Calculus
[13] Points shown are for the revised Institute of Financial Services Certificate in Financial Studies (CeFS) taught from September 2003
[14] Points shown are for the Institute of Financial Services Diploma in Financial Studies (DipFS) and come into effect for entry to higher education in 2008
[15] Points are awarded for the Certificate of Personal Effectiveness (COPE) awarded by ASDAN and CCEA
[16] Points for Advanced Extension Awards are over and above those gained from the A level grade
[17] Points for the Core are awarded only when a candidate achieves the Welsh Baccalaureate Advanced Diploma

UNIT GRADE INFORMATION

As a result of the increasing need to differentiate between the many well-qualified applicants for higher education, unit grade information for certificated qualifications (such as GCE AS and A level) will be supplied to higher education institutions. It is intended to give institutions greater depth of information about their applicants, in order to help them decide whether to make an offer and assess the strengths and weaknesses of applicants. This means that the grades you achieve in each unit of your qualification may start to matter, as well as your final overall grade.

There is space for you to fill in your unit grade scores on your UCAS application, and the information will also be made available by UCAS direct to institutions. Unit grades may be specified as part of conditional offers but it is not expected that this practice will be widespread. You should look at individual university and college prospectuses and websites and check entry requirements and entry profiles to find out their individual policies relating to unit grade information.

TARGETING THE RIGHT COURSES

Some institutions publish lists of subjects they recognise for admission purposes, and if you are taking, for example, two subjects from among Art, Design and Technology, and Communication Studies, this is well worth checking. A level General Studies is accepted by some departments, but not others. (It is more likely to be considered in the newer universities and in the colleges of further and higher education.)

Here are a few dos and don'ts to make sure that the final five courses you select are targeted to give you the best chance of success:

Do...

■ Carefully check the required entry grades and qualifications on the UCAS website or in *University and College Entrance Guide (The Big Book)*; then confirm this by checking the institution's prospectus or website or, preferably, by contacting them direct to make sure there is no chance you have misunderstood or that any changes have been made since the prospectuses were printed.

■ Check that the post-16 qualifications you have opted to take will give you the entry qualifications you need and that you are on track to achieve the right grades.

■ Be realistic about the grades you are likely to achieve.

■ Make sure you apply to at least one institution which is likely to give you a slightly lower offer, as a safety net.

Don't...

■ Apply to five popular institutions which all demand high grades. This is difficult to illustrate because the situation varies from subject to subject, and a good applicant may have little to fear. But beware, for example, of applying to study English at five universities such as, say, Durham, Nottingham, Oxford, UCL and York, because entry to study English in these particular universities is extremely competitive and, even with high predicted grades, you cannot be sure of acceptance. Better to name at least one university or college which is not so popular – preferably, one that makes offers at a slightly lower level.

■ Apply for lots of disparate subjects – you will have a difficult job justifying this in your personal statement and admissions tutors will question how genuine your interest is in each subject.

> Tip
>
> If you have (or are likely to achieve) less than the minimum qualifications for entry to an honours degree course, your qualification level may be suitable for entry to an HND course or foundation degree, which you can convert into a full degree with an additional year of study (see Chapter 4 for further information).

Resources

Publications:

■ *Choosing Your A Levels and Post-16 Options* (Trotman, www.trotman.co.uk)

■ *Choosing Your Degree Course & University* (Trotman, www.trotman.co.uk)

■ *Which Degree? 2007*, 2 volumes (Trotman, www.trotman.co.uk)

■ *Degree Course Offers 2008 entry* (Trotman, www.trotman.co.uk)

Websites:

■ www.crb.gov.uk – Criminal Records Bureau, with information about its disclosure service

■ www.disclosurescotland.co.uk – Scottish Criminal Record Office disclosure service

■ www.materials.ac.uk/resources/library/apelintro.asp – information about Accreditation of Prior Experiential Learning, including a downloadable document

- www.qca.org.uk/493.html – National Qualifications Framework
- www.ucas.com/candq/apl – information about Accreditation of Prior Learning

II

THE ADMISSIONS PROCEDURE – APPLICATIONS, INTERVIEWS, OFFERS AND BEYOND

7

APPLICATIONS AND OFFERS

MAKING YOUR APPLICATION

As the **calendar for advanced-level students** on pages 4–6 shows, if you are on a two-year sixth-form or college course, all your higher education research work should ideally be done by September/October of the second year – more than a year before you start in higher education. If you are on a one-year course, you are working to the same application deadlines, but still need to research your higher education options.

DEADLINES

The deadline for application to most subjects is **15 January**. (Remember, you will have to submit your application to your referee well before this). *All applications submitted by 15 January are considered* – however, it is advisable to apply as early as you can. This is because too many people apply after Christmas during the few weeks leading up to the 15 January deadline; those who apply earlier may therefore receive more detailed consideration by admissions tutors simply because the numbers being handled are fewer. Also, as time passes, entry standards often have to be tightened, and applicants more rigorously selected. If you are on a two-year sixth-form or college course, aim to submit your UCAS application to your referee by late November.

Some subjects have an earlier application deadline:

■ Applications for courses leading to professional qualifications in **medicine, dentistry or veterinary science** must be submitted by 15 October.

- Applications for all courses at Oxford or Cambridge Universities must be submitted by 15 October.
- Applications via Route B for art and design courses should be submitted by 24 March.

The procedure for these courses is covered in more detail in **Chapter 8**.

 Always make your application well before the advertised closing date.

WHAT HAPPENS NEXT?

UCAS will acknowledge your application and confirm the courses you have applied to – you must check that this information is correct, and contact UCAS (0871 468 0468) immediately if it is not. UCAS will also provide you with your **Personal ID (PID)**, **application number** and Track **username** and **password**. These will enable you to log in to the UCAS database and use Track (the online tracking system) to follow the progress of your application. Keep a careful note of your application number and, if you contact UCAS, universities or colleges, be prepared to quote it – this will save a lot of time and trouble.

DECISIONS AND OFFERS

Universities and colleges will inform UCAS of their decisions. You should log in to Track periodically to the check the status of your application. If you have entered a valid address, UCAS will email you to tell you that a change has been made to your application. The message will not specify whether you have received an offer or a rejection, but will ask you to log in to Track to find out.

Decisions will arrive in a random order, beginning a few weeks after you apply. You can also check your offers via Track on the UCAS website. If you have a long wait, it may mean that you are regarded as borderline (although this is not always the case). There are three main decisions:

- **U: unconditional offer** – No further qualifications are required. If you accept this offer then you are in!
- **C: conditional offer** – Still some work to do... But if you accept the offer and achieve the conditions in the examinations you are about to take, a place will be guaranteed.
- **R: unsuccessful** – Sorry – no place for you.

The following codes may also appear:

- **H: joint offer** – You may find that some universities and colleges with both degrees and HND courses in the same subject will send you a joint offer for both courses, but with different conditions (usually lower for the HND), so that you have an automatic insurance offer should you fail to achieve the results required for the degree. These joint offers count as only one, so you can hold both a firm degree/HND acceptance *and* an insurance offer if you wish (see below). However, you should note that if you miss the grades for the degree part of the firm offer but achieve the HND grades, you cannot take up your insurance choice instead.

- **W: withdrawn** – You have withdrawn this choice.
- **CNC: cancelled** – You have asked UCAS to cancel this choice.

Universities and colleges have to decide by 9 May whether or not to offer you a place (they are advised to make their decision by 31 March).

INTERVIEWS AND OPEN DAYS

Before they make a decision, institutions may wish to call you for interview. You should therefore be prepared to travel to universities or colleges during the winter; a Young Person's Railcard or a National Express Coachcard may be a good investment. Advice on preparing for interviews is given in **Chapter 9**. Alternatively you may be offered a conditional or unconditional place and invited to attend an open day.

REPLYING TO OFFERS

You have to reply to any offers you receive, but not until you have received decisions from all five of the institutions to which you applied. Once this has happened, you will be asked to reply to the offers you have received.

You can reply to your offers using Track on the UCAS website or by contacting the UCAS Customer Service Unit if you do not have access to the internet. (If you use Track, UCAS will receive your reply immediately.) You must reply to each offer with one of three options:

- **F: Firm Acceptance**: If you firmly accept an offer (either as **UF** if it is an unconditional offer, or **CF** if it is a conditional offer), this means that you are *sure* that the offer is your first preference of all the offers you have received through UCAS. If you get the grades, this will be the higher education course you take. You can make this reply once only; you will not be able subsequently to change or cancel your reply.
- **I: Insurance Acceptance**: If you have firmly accepted a conditional offer (CF), you may also hold one additional offer (either Conditional or Unconditional) as an Insurance acceptance (CI or UI). This is your fall-back, in case your grades are too low for your firm acceptance.
- **D: Decline**: If you decline an offer, you are indicating that you definitely do not wish to accept it.

You may accept a maximum of two offers (one firm and one conditional), so your combination of replies will be one of the following:

- Accept one offer firmly (UF or CF) and decline any others (D).
- Accept one offer firmly (CF) and one as an insurance (UI or CI), and decline any others (D).
- Decline all offers (D).

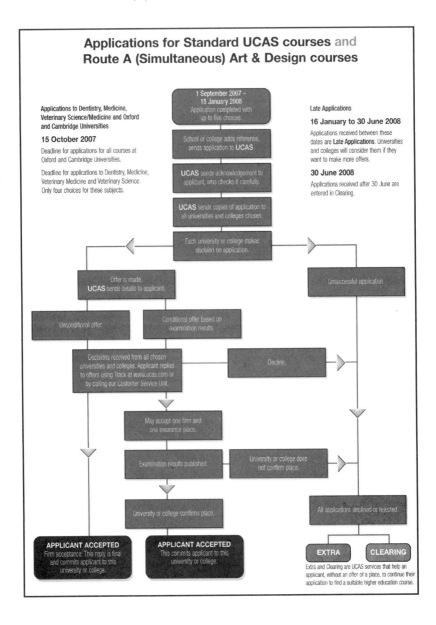

Applications for Standard UCAS courses and Route A (Simultaneous) Art & Design courses

If you firmly accept an *unconditional* offer of a place (UF), you are not entitled to choose an Insurance offer. If you firmly accept a *conditional* offer
(CF), then you may accept an *unconditional* offer as your Insurance (UI).

If one or more of your offers is a joint offer (H) for a degree *and* HND, your
reply will relate to the whole joint offer. You can choose to accept the joint
offer as a Firm or as an Insurance acceptance. Alternatively the joint offer can
be declined. You do not have the option at this stage to accept one part of the
joint offer and to decline the other.

The flowchart opposite may help you understand the options open to you.

> If you are applying for entry to courses in art and/or design, you must read
> the instructions published by UCAS very carefully since different application
> and reply procedures and dates may apply, depending on your choice of
> courses. See **Chapter 8** for more information.

TIPS ON MAKING YOUR DECISIONS

- **Consider your replies very carefully.** Ask for advice from your
  school or college tutor, or careers/Connexions adviser.
- Do not accept an offer (Firm or Insurance) unless you are sure that you
  will be happy to enrol on the course. The decisions you make are
  binding; **you are not permitted to alter your choices at a later
  stage**. (There is a commitment on the institution's part as well, to
  accept you if you fulfil the conditions.)
- It is advisable to choose as your Insurance acceptance an unconditional
  offer or one with conditions that are easier for you to meet than those of
  your Firm acceptance. (However, Apply does not disallow the opposite
  because, for example, courses do sometimes get cancelled.) If you have
  two offers such as AAB and ABB where the A in the latter is in a specified subject, you will need to weigh up which offer you are likely to find
  easiest to meet.
- Do not include as an Insurance acceptance a course which you would be
  unwilling to take up. If you are not accepted for your Firm choice and
  the Insurance offer is confirmed, you are committed to going there. It
  would be better not to hold an Insurance acceptance than to hold one
  you would not be willing to take up.
- Bear in mind the precise requirements of the offer. For example, if a
  BCC offer requires a B in a subject you are not very confident about,
  whereas an offer requiring higher grades overall does not specify the B in
  that subject, or perhaps lets you count general studies, then your
  Firm/Insurance decision needs to take these issues into account.

WHAT IF YOU DO NOT GET ANY OFFERS?

You may be able to make a further application via **Extra**, which begins in mid-March and ends in early July. You will be eligible to use Extra if you have used all five choices in your original application and you fulfil *any one* of the following criteria:

- You have had unsuccessful or withdrawal decisions for all your choices.
- You have cancelled your outstanding choices and hold no offers.
- You have received replies back from all five choices and have declined all offers made to you.

If you are eligible, UCAS will notify you of this. When you log on via Track, you will see that a special Extra button appears on your screen.

Courses that still have vacancies will be highlighted on the Course Search area of the UCAS website. (Alternatively, you can contact institutions direct.) When you enter the course details on your Track screen, a copy of your Extra application is sent automatically to the relevant university or college.

If you are made an offer, you can then choose whether or not to accept it. If you are currently studying for examinations, any offer that you receive is likely to be a conditional one, which will contain the required examination grades. If you decide to accept a conditional offer, you will not be able to take any further part in Extra. If you already have your examination results, you may receive an unconditional offer. Once you accept an unconditional offer you have that place.

If you are unsuccessful, decline an offer, or do not receive an offer within 21 days of choosing a course through Extra, you can make a further application via Extra (time permitting). The Extra button on your Track screen will be re-activated.

TIPS ON APPLYING VIA EXTRA

- Do some careful research, and seek guidance from your school, college or careers adviser and from the universities and colleges themselves.
- Think very carefully before applying again for the types of courses for which you have already been unsuccessful – it may simply result in another rejection.
- Be flexible – for example, if you applied to high-demand courses and institutions in your original application and were unsuccessful, you could consider related or alternative subjects.
- If you still do not succeed, you can find a place through Clearing (see **Chapter 10**).

8

Non-standard Applications

Applications for the majority of courses follow the pattern outlined in the previous chapters. However, there are some exceptions, specifically for:

■ Courses at Oxford and Cambridge Universities
■ Music conservatoires
■ Medicine, dentistry and veterinary science/medicine courses
■ Art and design courses
■ Deferred entry
■ Late applications.

Oxford and Cambridge

If you intend to apply for any course at either Oxford or Cambridge universities, the closing date for submitting your application is **15 October 2007**. You must also submit the Cambridge Application Form (CAF) or the Oxford Application Form (whichever is relevant) by this date. You can only apply to both Oxford *and* Cambridge if you already have a degree or will have gained one before September 2008. If not, you may apply for only one course at either Oxford or Cambridge. In-depth advice on making applications to these universities is given in *Getting Into Oxford & Cambridge* – see **Resources** at the end of the chapter.

Music conservatoires

Courses at the seven UK music conservatoires can be applied to online using the Conservatoires UK Admissions Service (CUKAS), which is run by UCAS and works in a similar way. However, unlike UCAS, applicants can still select six courses. The seven institutions are:

- Birmingham Conservatoire
- Leeds College of Music
- Royal College of Music
- Royal Northern College of Music
- Royal Scottish Academy of Music and Drama
- Royal Welsh College of Music and Drama
- Trinity College of Music.

The application deadline is **1 October 2007**, although late entries can be submitted if there are vacancies. Applicants registering on the CUKAS website will be able to access general advice, apply online and track their applications. Further information is available at www.cukas.ac.uk.

MEDICINE, DENTISTRY AND VETERINARY SCIENCE COURSES

If you intend to apply for a course leading to a professional qualification in medicine, dentistry or veterinary science/medicine, the closing date for submitting your application is **15 October 2007**. You are allowed to select a maximum of four courses in these subjects; if you list more than four, Apply will ask you to reduce your choices. The remaining space on your UCAS application may then be filled in with a course in another subject, should you so wish. There is strong competition for entry to medicine, dentistry and veterinary science/medicine courses and many people are necessarily disappointed in their first choice of study. In-depth advice on making applications in these subject areas is given in the *Getting Into* series – see **Resources** at the end of the chapter.

ART AND DESIGN COURSES

Universities and colleges can recruit to art and design courses via one or both of two equal pathways: Route A (Simultaneous) and Route B (Sequential). Use the UCAS website or *Trotman's Green Guides: Art, Design and Performing Arts Courses 2008* to identify those courses to be recruited through Route A and Route B respectively. Route B course codes always begin or end with the letter E and are clearly marked with a B on the **Course Search** area of the UCAS website.

Note that many courses will consider applicants through both routes. Route B is intended primarily for those students following an art and design foundation course – but foundation course students *can* gain places on courses through Route A.

Before deciding whether to apply through Route A and/or Route B you should take advice from your school, college, course tutor or careers/Connexions adviser.

ROUTE A (SIMULTANEOUS)

Route A applications are similar to the standard applications route (see previous chapter). You may apply for up to five courses and should submit your application between 1 September and the normal UCAS deadline (**15 January**). Copies of your application will be sent simultaneously to all Route A institutions you have selected.

Decisions on these applications will be due from institutions by 9 May 2008 and you will be advised of the date by which you must reply to any offers you receive. You will be able to accept any offers according to the normal UCAS rules, ie you will be able to hold one conditional offer firmly (CF) plus one offer (conditional or unconditional) as an insurance offer (CI or UI). If you have received unconditional offers you may only hold one of them firmly (UF).

Route A (Simultaneous) art and design application timetable	
1 September 2007	UCAS starts receiving applications for entry in autumn 2008.
15 January 2008	Last date for receipt of on-time application forms.
9 May 2008	Last date for universities to make decisions on applications received by 15 January.
Up to 6 June 2008	Applicants are required to reply to offers once all decisions have been received. The 'reply by' date depends on the date by which the last decision was received. Reply dates are printed on the 'Replying to offers' letters.
Mid-July 2008	Clearing starts.

ROUTE B (SEQUENTIAL)

In Route B, application forms should be submitted between 1 September 2007 and **24 March 2008**. You are advised to get your Route B application in by 7 March 2008. The normal UCAS online application is used but, in addition, you will be asked to give your order of preference for each Route B course you have chosen. Your application will then be sent to universities/colleges sequentially, in your stated order of preference.

Because of time constraints imposed by the sequential interview process, applicants choosing courses recruiting through this procedure are restricted to a maximum of three choices. Route B applicants can use their remaining

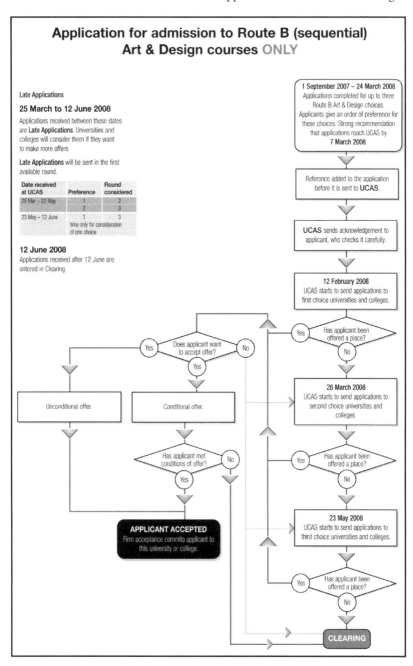

two choices for any courses recruited through the Route A procedure – see the section below on applying through both Route A (Simultaneous) and Route B (Sequential). You will receive decisions on your Route B applications according to the timetable below.

Route B (Sequential) art and design application timetable	
12 February 2008	UCAS starts to send applications in the first round to institutions.
24 March 2008	Last date for the receipt of on-time applications by UCAS. Applications received after this date will be stamped 'Late' and will receive a lower priority.
28 March 2008	UCAS starts to send applications in the second round to institutions.
9 May 2008	Last date for decisions from first-round institutions. UCAS will reject by default any decisions still outstanding.
23 May 2008	UCAS starts to send applications in the third round to institutions.
6 June 2008	Last date for decisions from second-round institutions. UCAS will reject by default any decisions still outstanding.
7 July 2008	Last date for decisions from third-round instititutions. UCAS will reject by default any decisions still outstanding.
Mid-July 2008	Clearing starts.

You will be given 14 calendar days in which to reply to offers. If replies are not received by the due date, the offers will lapse. The reply date will be advised in the offer letter.

If you are made an offer by your first choice and you accept it, your application will not be sent to subsequent choices. If your first choice does not make you an offer, your application will be forwarded to your second choice and so on.

Only one offer may be held in Route B, ie either an unconditional offer firmly accepted (UF) or a conditional offer firmly accepted (CF).

APPLICATIONS THROUGH BOTH ROUTES (ROUTE A AND ROUTE B)
As outlined above, art and design applicants may apply to up to five courses, but only three of these via Route B. This means that many applicants choose to apply to courses via both Route A and Route B, so that all five of their course choices are used. You can mix and match your Route A and Route B applications as you wish; the only constraint is that there is a maximum of

three Route B choices. Your Route A choices may therefore be for art and design courses or for any other subjects. For example, you could apply for one history and two art and design courses through Route A and two art and design courses through Route B.

If you want to apply for courses through both Route A and Route B, you should submit your Route A UCAS application by 15 January. The application allows you to indicate that you will want to add choices for consideration through Route B later (although of course this will only be possible if you have not already used all five choices through Route A).

You will be able to add Route B choices and declare an interview preference on Track on the UCAS website. You will also be able to provide an updated personal statement, if you would like to do so.

If you apply through Route A and subsequently add choices under Route B you will receive decisions as follows:

Route A	Decisions will be received up to 9 May as described above. However, there will be no facility to reply to offers through Route A until your application has been considered through Route B.
	If you have received offers through Route A which you wish to accept, you may cancel the Route B application in order to reply to those offers.
Route B	On receipt of an offer from a Route B choice, you will receive a letter which will set out all options open to you. You will be expected to reply within 14 calendar days.
	You may hold two offers (CF plus CI or UI) across Routes A and B but only *one* offer from the Route B choices.

You may hold Route A and Route B offers in the following combinations:

Route A	UF	None	CF+CI	CF+UI	CF	CF	CI	UI
Route B	None	UF	None	None	CI	UI	CF	CF

Notes:
1 | Only one offer may be held in Route B.
2 | Two offers (CF plus CI or UI) may be held in Route A, according to normal UCAS rules.
3 | Two offers (any combination) may be held across Routes A and B.
4 | Only one UF offer may be held, according to normal UCAS rules.
5 | It is possible to hold a CF in one Route without an insurance in either.

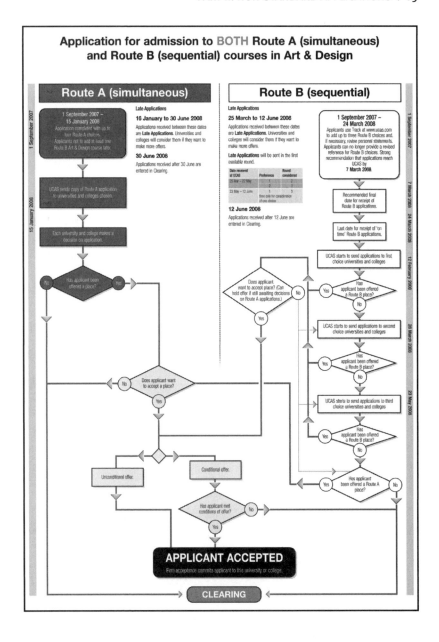

What happens next?

As for all applications, conditional offers will be confirmed as soon as you have obtained the required qualification. The standard Clearing procedure operates for applicants via both routes – see **Chapter 10** for more information.

DEFERRED ENTRY

Gap years are an increasingly popular option for many students – they offer a unique opportunity to broaden horizons and/or (as the cost of higher education continues to rise) to save some money while gaining valuable experience in the workplace. If you do plan, for whatever reason, to defer your entry into higher education until 2009, there are three options available to you – each is listed below with a few notes on the pros and cons.

OPTION 1 – APPLY VIA UCAS FOR DEFERRED ENTRY

You can make your application this year (2007–8) and select a start date of 2009 in your UCAS application to indicate that you wish to defer your entry (see **Chapter 14**). The major advantage of this option is that you get the formalities out of the way while you are still at school or college and available for interview – then you can relax.

Generally speaking, applications for deferred entry are dealt with in the normal way, but do be aware that for some subjects (such as medicine, certain science/maths subjects and professional subjects), admissions tutors may be a little cautious about offering you a place. It is therefore important to be sure you really want to defer before using this option, and to check with the department you are thinking of applying to whether they are happy to admit you a year later.

Remember that if you *do* apply for entry in 2009, but find that you have no useful way of spending the interim year after all, the institution is not obliged to take you a year earlier (in 2008).

If you choose to defer, remember to mention your reasons and plans for your year out in the Statement section of Apply (see **Chapter 17**) as this is much more likely to make institutions more amenable to giving you a deferred place.

OPTION 2 – APPLY VIA UCAS FOR STANDARD ENTRY

If you are not confident enough of your decision to tick the 'deferred entry' box on your UCAS application, you can apply for the normal admission year and, later on, ask the higher education institution where you are accepted whether you can defer. This means you do not need to say anything on your UCAS form about deferred entry until your plans are really firm – but, on the other hand, the institution is quite entitled to say that the place it has offered you is for 2008 entry only, and you must either take it up or apply all over again for entry in 2009.

OPTION 3 – DO NOT APPLY VIA UCAS UNTIL THE FOLLOWING YEAR

It is possible to delay applying to UCAS until *after* you have received your results – meaning that you make your UCAS application during your gap year. This can be a good option in some instances, especially if your exam results turn out to be significantly different from those you were predicted. Your grades are also guaranteed, and if you accept an offer it will be a firm decision, so institutions may consider you a better bet than a candidate who is only predicted those grades. The disadvantage though is that you must find time *during your gap year* to get your research up to date, fill in your UCAS application and (possibly) attend open days and interviews. This can limit your gap-year options – you will need to be contactable at all times, and flying back from Down Under to attend an interview could make a serious dent in your finances.

MAKING A LATE APPLICATION

All Route A applications should be submitted before 15 January. **Avoid applying late if you can.** Many popular courses fill up, and getting a place will be more difficult, if not impossible.

However, if you decide you would like to apply to higher education after 15 January, you still can. Up to **30 June**, UCAS will send your application to your named institutions, but they will only consider you at their discretion. *If* they do choose to consider you, the same procedures are followed as for a normal application, and you will reply to offers in the usual way.

Applications received between 1 July and **20 September** will be processed through the Clearing scheme which operates in July, August and September.

Resources

Publications:
- *Getting Into Art & Design Courses* (Trotman, www.trotman.co.uk)
- *Getting Into Dental School* (Trotman, www.trotman.co.uk)
- *Getting Into Medical School* (Trotman, www.trotman.co.uk)
- *Getting Into Oxford & Cambridge* (Trotman, www.trotman.co.uk)
- *Getting Into Veterinary School* (Trotman, www.trotman.co.uk)
- *Trotman's Green Guides: Art, Design and Performing Arts Courses 2008* (Trotman, www.trotman.co.uk)
- *Trotman's Green Guides: Healthcare Courses 2008* (Trotman, www.trotman.co.uk)

Websites:
- **www.cukas.ac.uk**
- **www.admissions.ox.ac.uk/apply** – for information on applications to Oxford
- **www.cam.ac.uk/admissions/undergraduate/apply** – for information on applications to Cambridge and to download a copy of the Cambridge Application Form

9

INTERVIEWS AND SELECTION

WHY DO ADMISSIONS TUTORS INTERVIEW CANDIDATES?

Realistically, tutors seek able students with academic potential, in sufficient numbers to fill the places on their courses. In deciding which applicants to accept, selectors are looking for:

- **Intellectual ability** – Can you cope with the academic and professional demands of the subject and course?
- **Motivation** – Are you aware, purposeful and realistic about yourself, with clear reasons for applying?
- **Competitive applicants** – How well do you compare with other applicants for the course?
- **Applicants who are likely to accept** – If offered a place, is there a good chance you will accept it?
- **Students who will make a contribution** – Will you get involved in the life of the higher education institution and contribute in lectures, practicals and tutorials?
- **Applicants who are likely to get the grades** – Are you expected to achieve the level of grades in your exams that this course generally commands?

They may be able to glean much of this information from your personal statement (see **Chapter 17**) but some will also use interviews to help them decide which applicants to make an offer to. Fewer applicants are interviewed today than a few years ago – partly because of the increased numbers of potential entrants. However, interviews are still used:

- For borderline candidates (give it your best shot as many admissions tutors like to give applicants a chance, even when doubtful if you will make the grade).
- To distinguish between large numbers of similar, very able applicants. (This is particularly likely if you are applying for very competitive courses, for example at Oxbridge or in veterinary medicine.)

WHAT WILL YOU BE ASKED?

Interviews can take different forms – you could find yourself on your own in front of an interview panel, or as part of a group, being observed as you carry out a particular task. You may even be asked to take a written test. Interview questions can be wide-ranging and unpredictable – but, on the other hand, there are a few 'old chestnuts' that tend to come up over and over again. It is wise to have considered how you might respond to predictable questions like:

- Why this subject?
- Why this department or faculty?
- Why this university or college?
- What can *you* bring to university?

You should also be prepared to talk about:

- Your advanced-level study (What particularly interests you? What additional reading and research have you done?)
- Topical issues related to your chosen subject (read the newspapers, watch the news and search the internet for the latest stories on genetic research, legal or political problems, government policy and so on, depending on your subject)
- Anything you mention in your personal statement.

PREPARING YOURSELF

Obviously you should not memorise or recite answers to any of the questions above – but think through the kind of things you would like to say. Taking the question *What can* you *bring to university?* as an example, you could:

- Talk about your strengths, interests and ambitions, particularly with reference to courses you are interested in.

- Mention anything a bit individual or a little different, that you can bring to share with others (for example, you may have debating experience, a French background, great rugby skills, extensive practice in ornithology or orienteering/navigation expertise. Or you may have developed mentoring skills through your work as a sixth-form or college ambassador to feeder schools).

It is a good idea to ask your school or college to give you a mock interview – this can be an excellent way of preparing yourself to think on your feet and answer unseen questions.

You should start thinking about interviews as early as possible; for example, as you consider your course choices and construct a shortlist of higher education institutions to apply to, you should research answers to the questions admissions tutors might ask. If the admissions tutor comes up with 'Why this university or college?', you will then remember their particularly strong facilities or the unique angle of the course.

Try to keep interviews in mind as you write your personal statement (see **Chapter 17**). It is very likely that interviewers will draw on it for their questions, so do not mention anything you cannot elaborate on. Conversely, if you have a particular passion or area of interest in your chosen subject that you are just dying to talk about, make sure you mention it in your statement.

TOP TIPS FOR INTERVIEWS
- Dress smartly, smile and stand up straight.
- Give eye contact and do not fidget.
- Do your best to appear thoughtful, committed and genuinely interested in your chosen subject.
- Always have one or two prepared questions of your own about the course, opportunities after you graduate or a relevant academic topic. (Try not to ask questions only on topics covered in material already published and sent to you by the university or college.)

More detailed advice on interview technique and possible interview questions is given in the *Getting Into* series (see **Resources** section below).

Resources

Publications:
- *Degree Course Offers 2008* – gives subject-specific interview advice and questions (Trotman, www.trotman.co.uk)
- *Getting In Getting On 2008* (UCAS, www.ucasbooks.com)

■ The *Getting Into* series – gives in-depth advice on all aspects of admissions for a range of subjects including Art & Design, Business & Management, Dentistry, Law, Oxford & Cambridge, Medicine, Physiotherapy, Psychology and Veterinary Science (Trotman, www.trotman.co.uk)

10

EXAM RESULTS AND CLEARING

Most applicants are accepted conditionally, so the results of exams taken or assessments completed in May/June are very important.

BEFORE RESULTS DAY

After you have taken your exams, you deserve to relax but it is worth giving some thought to what you will do if you do not get the grades needed for your higher education place – a sort of 'Plan B'. Will you try to secure a place through Clearing (see page 75)? Would you rather retake and apply again next year for the course you really wanted? Or are you having doubts about whether higher education is really for you?

If you are ill or have some other problem that you think may adversely affect your results, tell the institutions whose offers you are holding, or ask your school or college to contact them on your behalf. You may need to get a doctor's note to support your case. Admissions tutors will do their best to take adverse circumstances into account, but they must know about them *before* your results come out. If you leave it until after you have disappointing results, it may be too late.

> You *must* arrange your holidays so that you are at home when the results are published. Even if all goes well and your grades are acceptable, you need to confirm your place and deal with your registration, accommodation and loan. If not, you need to take advice, find out about course vacancies, and reach some quick decisions about possible offers of places in the Clearing system.

RESULTS DAY

A level results are issued on 21 August 2008 (Scottish Highers a week earlier). UCAS will supply examination results direct to the institutions for the majority of applicants taking the following examinations or courses:

- GCE A levels and AS levels
- BTEC National Awards, Certificates and Diplomas
- SQA Advanced Highers, Highers, Intermediate 2 and Core Skills
- Irish Leaving Certificate
- Welsh Baccalaureate Advanced Diploma
- International Baccalaureate
- CACHE Diploma
- Music examinations (grades 6–8)
- IFS Certificate in Financial Services Practice.

You should supply your results in these examinations to the institutions only if asked to do so, except that you can avoid possible delays if you send your BTEC results to the institutions as soon as you receive them.

If you have taken any other exams, such as SCE standard grade, GCSE or overseas qualifications, you must send your results to those institutions where you are holding offers as soon as you receive them.

When your results are released, and have been received by the institutions, admissions tutors will compare your results with the conditions they set and make a decision on whether to accept you.

 You can check institutions' decisions on results day via Track.

IF YOU GOT THE GRADES...

Congratulations! Your place will be confirmed; a university or college cannot reject you if you have met the conditions of your offer. Before the end of August, UCAS will send you an official notification that your place is confirmed, and you will be asked to send your reply to the institution within 14 days (the latest date for receipt of the reply is printed on the letter).

Make sure you get from the university or college the information you will need about:

- Accommodation
- Term dates
- Introductory arrangements.

Some institutions send you this material as soon as you accept firmly; some, only if you ask for it and a few, later in the procedure (even after your results). Check in good time.

IF YOU MISSED OUT...

Do not panic! **You should contact the institutions immediately to find out if they will accept you anyway.** This is because admissions tutors may decide to confirm your offer, even if you failed to meet some of the conditions. It has been known for applicants to be accepted on much lower grades if there are places available, there is good school or college support and, perhaps, a good interview record, although this varies greatly from course to course. Alternatively, you may be offered a place on a different course.

Before the end of August, UCAS will send you an official notification of the result of your application. If you have been offered a place on an alternative course, you will have a choice of actions. These will be listed on the notification letter.

If the institution does not confirm your offer, you can find a place through Clearing (see below) or, alternatively, you can retake your exams and apply again the following year.

CLEARING

Do not panic if you do not get the grades you had hoped for and your offer is not confirmed. If you're flexible and you have reasonable exam results, there is still a good chance you could find another course through Clearing, which helps those without a place to find one. You are eligible for Clearing if you paid the full £15 application fee and:

- You have not withdrawn from the UCAS system.
- You are not holding any offers (either because you did not receive any, or because you declined the offers you did receive).
- Your offers have not been confirmed because you have not met the conditions (such as not achieving the required grades).
- You made your UCAS application too late for it to be considered in the normal way (after 30 June for standard applications; after 12 June for Route B art and design courses).

UCAS is creating an electronic replacement to its 'Clearing passport' for 2008 entry. At the time of going to press, this was at an early stage of development, but it will still involve applicants each having a Clearing number so that they can contact relevant institutions.

WHAT DO I HAVE TO DO?

You need to search the lists of courses with vacancies to see if there are any that interest you. Course vacancies are published from the middle of August until late September. Arrangements for the publication of vacancies vary from year to year and precise sources of guidance for the summer of 2008 will be announced by UCAS closer to the time. In 2007, for example, official lists of vacancies will be published in these places:

■ The UCAS website (www.ucas.com/clearing)
■ Some newspapers (the *Independent*, the *Independent on Sunday*, and others to be confirmed).

Official helplines are also a useful source of information and advice – try the BBC Student One Life Helpline on 0808 100 8000.

Make a list of the courses that interest you, and contact the institutions in rank order of your preference to ask if they will accept you. It is recommended that you telephone, email or call in person because the admissions tutor will want to speak to you personally, not to a parent or teacher. Keep your Clearing number to hand as you will probably be asked for it.

 You need to be available in person to deal with admissions tutors and make decisions. Plan your summer holiday so you are at home when your exam results come out.

If you're not convinced that a course is right for you, remember that you do not have to commit yourself. Only when you are certain you have found the right course should you accept an offer of a place.

Top tips on Clearing

■ Talk to your careers adviser about which courses and subjects would be most suitable for you, particularly if your original UCAS application was unsuccessful.
■ Remember that you can apply for any course that has places left – you do not need to keep to the same subjects which you first applied for. If you do decide to apply for courses that are quite different from the ones you originally selected, make sure you do your research very thoroughly, referring back to prospectuses and websites.

■ Although you will have to act quickly, do not make any hasty decisions; only accept an offer if you are sure the course is right for you.

■ One way of making sure you are happy with your choice of course is to go to the university or college in person, because the best way to find out more is to pay it a visit. Most institutions are happy to make arrangements to meet applicants and show them around, and many will have open days. They know that you could be spending the next three or four years there, and that you want to be sure you are making the right choice.

■ If you are applying for art and design courses, you may need to supply a portfolio of work as well as your Clearing number.

■ Remember that institutions are likely to refer back to your UCAS application when deciding whether to make you an offer – you may want to have another look at what you wrote on your personal statement to make sure you are familiar with it, just in case an admissions tutor wants to ask you about it.

The diagram overleaf gives tips on what you might do if you do not get a place through Clearing.

RETAKES

Remember, disappointing results need not mean the end of your ambitions. If low grades have prevented your acceptance on a course of your choice, you may consider retaking your exams. For example, in some A level subjects, and with some syllabuses, this is possible in November or in January following your June exams. Alternatively, you may need to spend a full year retaking and, in that case, you could consider changing to an A level subject where you have greater aptitude and a better chance of achieving high grades.

While most university and college departments consider retake candidates – and some welcome the greater maturity and commitment to hard work that retaking demonstrates – be aware that you may be asked for higher grades. It is always worth checking with the relevant admissions tutor that your proposed retake programme is acceptable. It is very rare for Oxford or Cambridge to accept applicants who have retaken their exams.

WHAT TO DO IF YOU DON'T GET A PLACE THROUGH CLEARING

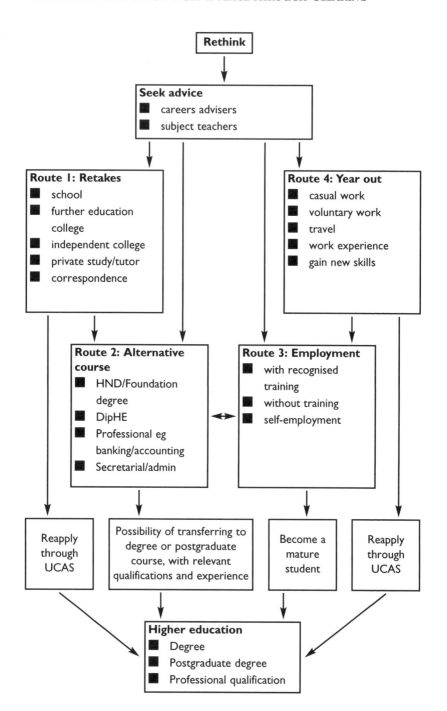

III

USING APPLY TO SUBMIT YOUR UCAS APPLICATION

11

INTRODUCING APPLY

Apply is the online application system. It is found at www.ucas.com/apply. As well as being easy and convenient to use, it:

- Speeds up the processing of higher education applications.
- Incorporates checks that prevent you from making simple errors.
- Is supported by the very latest UCAS course data and relevant additional information.

This chapter provides a brief outline of the Apply process, giving you guidelines on setting up your account, together with tips to make the application process as easy as possible. The remaining chapters of this book work through each section of the online application form.

GETTING STARTED

USING APPLY VIA A SCHOOL OR COLLEGE

In June of each year, UCAS coordinators at every registered school, college, careers and Connexions centre are sent an Apply package, with a specific website address (URL), username and password. Your UCAS coordinator registers your centre to use Apply and sets up a unique *buzzword* made up of at least six letters and numerals. This buzzword is then passed on to you and all UCAS applicants at your centre.

Tip The buzzword allows you to log on to Apply, and allows UCAS to see which centre you are from. When you enter your buzzword, do not hit the return key. Use the **next** button or the buzzword will not be accepted.

You can access the Apply system from any computer with internet access. You will move through to the registration screen, and you will be asked to provide personal details including first names, surname, title, sex, date of birth, address, telephone numbers and email address. Apply will check your details with you (they will automatically be entered into the **Personal Details** section of your application, where you will have the opportunity to change them later). You will be asked to enter your buzzword. When you press **next**, you will then be provided with your own username, which will appear on screen, and asked to choose a unique password and select four security questions with answers. You can then enter these details to log on and use Apply at any time and in any place where there is access to the internet, from Thailand to Tyneside.

USING APPLY AS AN INDIVIDUAL

If you want to apply to study on a higher education course, but are not attached to a school or college, you can – quite easily from anywhere with access to the internet – make an application using the UCAS online Apply system.

To log in, click on **Apply** on the UCAS website, and then select the relevant links to the left of the screen. When you have read through the guidance, you can register from the Apply homepage. Select **2008 login**. You will be asked to choose a password and a security question and answer. You will then be issued – on screen – with a username that you must note down and keep secure. Then you will be asked to answer a set of straightforward eligibility questions in order to start your application.

After this, the only difference between making an application as an individual and making it via a school is that **individual applicants are responsible for entering their own reference** (see **Chapter 18**). Your reference must be written by a responsible person, who knows you well enough to comment on your suitability for higher education and who can supply a valid email address or phone number. This could be an employer, a senior colleague in employment or voluntary work, a trainer, a careers adviser or the teacher of a relevant further education course you have recently attended. Your referee cannot be a friend or a relative. You may only supply one reference, and you should save it in electronic format ready to paste into Apply.

Because individuals' UCAS applications are sent direct to UCAS (rather than to a referee at school or college), it is a good idea to use the **view all** function to view your form and print out a copy to keep before submitting it to UCAS. Should you encounter difficulties at any stage, there is help on the Apply area of the UCAS website, or you can seek advice from the UCAS Customer Service Unit on 0871 468 0468 between 8.30am and 6pm on weekdays.

TECHNICAL REQUIREMENTS

To be able to access and use Apply, your computer set-up needs to comply with the following:

- You need to be operating Internet Explorer version 5 or higher, or Netscape Navigator 6 or higher. (Older versions of web browsers are less secure and can cause problems when you attempt to access secure websites such as Apply.)
- Your browser must have 128-bit encryption enabled.
- Your browser must have JavaScript enabled.
- Your monitor should be 15 inches or larger.
- Your display should be set to at least 256 colours.
- Your screen should be set to a resolution of 800x600 or above.

If you are unsure about any of these points, consult your computer manual or help facility.

Most web browsers will 'cache' the web pages you view. This means that they will be temporarily stored on your computer to help speed up your movements between the pages you wish to view (because your computer will not have to spend the time reloading previously viewed pages from the remote source). However, in some instances, caching of web pages will not allow you to update your data in Apply. To avoid this scenario and to ensure that pages are reloaded every time you view them, you should check the following settings on your web browser:

- **Netscape versions 6 and above**: Choose edit from the toolbar at the top of the browser. From the subsequent menu, select preferences. Then go to advanced; then cache. Under the heading 'Document in cache is compared to document on network', ensure the option every time is chosen.
- **Internet Explorer versions 5 and above**: Choose tools from the toolbar at the top of the browser. From the subsequent menu, select internet options. Click on the settings button under temporary internet files. Under the heading 'Check for newer versions of stored pages', ensure the option every visit to the page is chosen.

NAVIGATING APPLY

On the registration screen, you can select English or Welsh from a dropdown list. After that, you can use the Options/Opsiynau link in the left-hand navigation bar at any time to change the language. When you log on, you will be taken to the Apply main screen, illustrated overleaf.

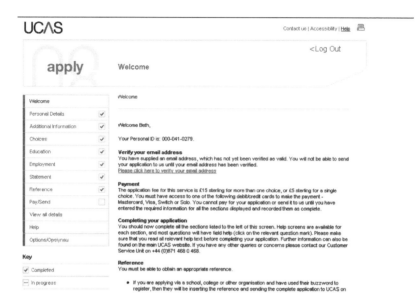

Apply is divided into the following sections:

- **Personal Details**
- **Additional Information**
- **Choices**
- **Education**
- **Employment**
- **Statement**.

You can access each section by clicking on its name to the left of the screen. There are on-screen instructions in every section, guiding you through what you have to do. If you get stuck at any point, you can access help text by clicking on the **Help** button or by clicking on the question mark next to each section. The text relates directly to the task you are completing at that point in time.

Some screens in Apply have **next** and **previous** buttons allowing you to move from page to page. You must use these, as the **back** and **forward** buttons on your web browser are not visible. Every now and then, you may be presented with an error screen telling you that the page hasn't been found and suggesting that you click **refresh**. Do not panic; just right-click on the screen and select **refresh**. The page should then be restored and you can continue as normal.

You are free to move between sections as you like, leaving them partially completed (in progress) and returning to them later if necessary. Just tick the 'section completed' box and then click on save when each area is complete.

When you click on save, any inaccurate or missing information will be highlighted in green to indicate that it is not yet complete. Even if you confirm that the section is finished, you can still return to it and add additional information if you need to.

 | Remember to save all your changes.

CHECKING THE PROGRESS OF YOUR APPLICATION

The status of your application is displayed on the left of the screen. It shows whether each section of Apply is 'not started', 'in progress' or 'complete'. A red tick next to each section shows that a section is complete.

At any stage while you're using Apply you can click on view all to preview or print a copy of your application in a viewer-friendly format. This will enable you to check through what you've done quickly and easily. Any incomplete sections will be highlighted in green.

You will not be able to submit your application until every section of Apply is complete. Once you have finished your application, agreed to the UCAS declaration and sent it to your referee, the status of your application will appear at one of the following stages, every time you log on:

- Application not checked
- Application checked
- Reference not yet started
- Reference in progress
- Reference awaiting approval
- Application sent to UCAS
- Your application number is...

Once you have your application number and password, you can continue to check the status of your application using Track.

SECURITY TIPS

For data protection reasons, Apply is a secure area of the UCAS website. More recent web browsers have a built-in feature allowing you to save your password so that you do not have to remember or retype it later. However, if you use this facility it will allow anyone using that particular computer to log on to your account and change the details of your application. For this reason it is strongly recommended that you do *not* use this feature.

When you have finished a session using Apply, it is strongly recommended that you log out properly by using the Log out button (*not* by simply closing the window you are in). Once you have logged out you should close your web browser down completely. This will ensure that no one will be able to access your details.

HOW THE REST OF THIS BOOK WORKS

The remaining chapters of this book will take you step-by-step through each section of Apply, giving you general advice on the nature of the information asked of you and the basic principles of getting it right. Each area of Apply has a corresponding chapter in this book:

- Personal details – basic facts such as name, address and date of birth
- Additional information (for UK applicants only) – mostly data for equal opportunities monitoring
- Courses – your selection of institutions and subjects
- Education – your school/college details and exams, past and future
- Employment – any jobs that you have held
- Statement – the most important section, your personal statement.

In each section, the subheadings relate directly to the headings used in Apply, so you can easily locate the relevant information.

The final part of the book deals with finishing off your application, including information on:

- Declaration – your agreement with UCAS and institutions
- Submitting your application
- Fee payment
- Reference.

At the end of the book you will find a section on **Troubleshooting** (see **Chapter 19**) which will help you solve some of the most frequently encountered problems. Further help is available via the 'Help' text accessible on individual Apply screens, and in guidance on the UCAS website.

STOP AND THINK!

Before you start your application, here are some last-minute tips and reminders...

- Make sure you have done all your research thoroughly and you are happy with your choices. If in doubt, take another look at the **In the think tank** section of this book.
- Collect together the following:
  - ☐ Your personal details
  - ☐ All school or college attendance dates
  - ☐ Exam results slips and entry forms
  - ☐ Any employment details
  - ☐ Details of the higher education courses you are applying for, including institution and course codes (you can find these via Course Search on the UCAS website).
- Read carefully through the guidance available on the Apply homepage.
- Be honest and truthful – you must be able to back up all your statements.
- Do not try to make more than one application in the same year.
- Remember that once your application reaches UCAS, you cannot amend it or add anything to it.

You should now be ready to start your application –
read on and good luck!

12

PERSONAL DETAILS

Obviously, UCAS and the universities and colleges to which you are applying need to know who you are and where they can get hold of you. There is little use in applying if they do not! What is less obvious is that they will need to know about a number of other aspects of your life. This can be for important financial reasons (eg who assesses your eligibility for funding) or to determine whether you require any additional support whilst studying, for example, if you have a disability. As such, your application will contain quite a lot of information about you, which we will deal with here.

You may already have entered some of it when you registered for Apply – this information will have been transferred into the **Personal Details** section of the application, where you may amend it.

Specifically, this section covers:

- Personal:
  - ☐ Name, gender and address
  - ☐ Telephone numbers, email address and date of birth
  - ☐ Residential category and nationality
- Student support:
  - ☐ Fee code
  - ☐ Student support arrangements
- Mailings from UCAS
- Nominated access
- Criminal convictions
- Disability/special needs

PERSONAL

The information you entered when you registered will have been drawn through into the **registration details** part of your application. You can edit or alter it at this stage.

NAME, GENDER AND ADDRESS

Whatever you give as your title, name and address will form the basis of your UCAS and university or college record. Although it may sound surprising, every year there are a number of applicants who make elementary errors when entering their own **names**! The following example is fine:

Title	Ms
Surname/Family name	Jones
First/Given name(s)	Rachel

The example below, however, will cause problems (and a lot of people do this):

Title	Mr
Surname/Family name	Robarts
First/Given name(s)	Mark Robarts

Sorry, Mark – but for ever afterwards, you will be Mr M R Robarts to UCAS and the institutions to which you are applying.

If your name is not easily divided into surname and first names decide how you want to be addressed, and stick to it. For example:

Title	Mr
Surname/Family name	Nik A Kamal Hassan
First/Given name(s)	

Chinese students, whose own custom is to put the family name first, will normally have to accept being addressed in the western style – so the following example will appear as C H A Wong:

Title	Ms
Surname/Family name	Wong
First/Given name(s)	Chu-Hai Angela

It is just possible that institutions may address you as Wong Chu-Hai, but do not count on it. If you have adopted a western name, feel free to include it.

 Do not provide nicknames. It is important that you enter the same names that appear on official documents, such as exam certificates.

For **gender**, you are asked to choose 'the option that best describes your gender'. In other words, you are not restricted to selecting your biological sex.

The **address** section should not present you with any particularly challenging problems. Your postal address is the one that will appear in the UCAS record, and is where correspondence about your application will be sent. This does not have to be your home address; you are at liberty to have your letters sent anywhere you choose – your school, for example.

If you do decide to give your school address, you will need to tell UCAS to send correspondence to your home address, or another more suitable location, once you leave – UCAS will not do this automatically. (Tell your university or college as well.) If you do not inform UCAS, offers of places or details of Clearing opportunities will be sent to your school. This will mean a delay in you receiving them and you could lose a place as a result.

In all instances, it is very important that you include your postcode as UCAS pre-sorts its letters for the Post Office by using the postcode, and correspondence with you might be delayed if you do not put it on your application.

TELEPHONE NUMBERS, EMAIL ADDRESS AND DATE OF BIRTH

Include your home telephone number, mobile number and email address if you have them, or access to them. Some admissions tutors prefer to communicate electronically, and it can speed up communication dramatically at Confirmation and Clearing time.

Make sure you include the area code in your home number, but do not use brackets or '+'. If it is an overseas number, remember to include the international dialling code.

Your date of birth is required for UCAS and institutions' records: select the day, month and year from the dropdown lists. Apply is designed to ensure that you cannot put in the wrong date. If you enter a date that does not exist, you will be told and will have to re-enter the information. The Apply system will then automatically enter your age on 1 September 2008 (the date of entry to higher education).

RESIDENTIAL CATEGORY AND NATIONALITY

Indicating whether your **permanent home** is within the UK or not should be straightforward. **Area of permanent residence** is less so. If you live:

- *Outside the UK* – name the country (eg Australia)
- *In Scotland* – name the district or islands area (eg Clackmannanshire)

- *In Greater London*– name the London borough (eg Bexley)
- *In a former metropolitan district* – name the district (eg Sefton)
- *Elsewhere in the UK* – name the county (eg Northamptonshire).

Apply provides a pop-up list of counties and boroughs for you to choose from if you answered 'Yes' to 'Is your permanent home in the UK?', and a list of countries if you answered 'No'.

 If you cannot find your area on the list, you need to look through the existing options to find one that matches your circumstances.

Your **country of birth** and **nationality** should present no problems, although it is worth mentioning that if you were born in the UK, you should select 'United Kingdom' for the former and 'UK national' for the latter (ie you cannot select 'Scotland', 'English' etc). This information is for statistical purposes only, to find out where applicants come from. It will not be used for selection purposes.

If your country of birth is not within the UK, you will also have to indicate your date of first entry to live in the UK. Using the dropdown lists, you should enter the date when you entered, or propose to enter, the UK.

Residential category can be more complicated, but is particularly important because what you enter here will be the point from which institutions will start to classify you as *home* or *overseas* for the purpose of tuition fees. Those classified as overseas pay a *much* higher annual tuition fee, which will usually be around £8000 and, for some courses, up to £20,000 by 2008. (Your tuition fee status has no direct connection with your nationality. It depends on your place of ordinary residence and the length of time you have been ordinarily resident there.)

You must choose from a list of residential category options, summarised below.

A   You are a UK or EU national, or are the child of a UK or EU national, and have lived in the European Economic Area (EEA) and/or Switzerland for three years, but not just for full-time education. If you are a UK national, you may also have lived in the Channel Islands and/or the Isle of Man during these three years.

B   You have Indefinite Leave to Enter or Remain in the UK or have the Right of Abode in the UK and have lived in the UK, the Channel Islands and/or the Isle of Man for three years, but not just for full-time education. However, this does not apply if you are exempt from immigration control, for example as a diplomat or a member of visiting armed forces or an employee of an international organisation or the family of such a person. If this is your situation, your residential category is O.

C You are a refugee, or have been granted Exceptional Leave to Enter or Remain, Humanitarian Protection or Discretionary Leave in the UK following an application for asylum, and you have lived in the UK, the Channel Islands or the Isle of Man since that status was recognised or granted, or you are such a person's husband, wife or child.

D You are an EEA or Swiss national, you live in the UK and you are a migrant worker (or you are such a person's husband, wife or child), and you have lived in the EEA and/or Switzerland for three years, but not just for full-time education.

G You would otherwise meet the criteria of categories A, B, C or D, but you have been living outside the UK, Channel Islands, Isle of Man, EEA and/or Switzerland, as applicable, because you, your husband or wife, or your parent have been temporarily working outside the area in question.

O Other.

You should take extra care that you enter the correct category. The help text in Apply has a series of questions that can help you to choose the right category. If you find this section difficult to complete as (for example) you live overseas because of your parents' work, classify yourself as best you can, and be prepared for questions from the institutions. They will try to be fair to you, but they do have a duty to apply the regulations justly to all their students. You could, before applying, write to institutions outlining your circumstances. Some overseas companies have standard letters for employees to use. It sometimes happens that universities and colleges will classify the same student in different ways, depending on their reading of the rules.

STUDENT SUPPORT

Use the dropdown list next to 'Fee code' to select which code applies to you. The list below will help you decide which code to choose:

01 Entire cost of tuition fees paid by private finance

02 Applying for student support assessment by local authority, Student Awards Agency for Scotland (SAAS) or Northern Ireland Education and Library Board, EU team, or Channel Islands or Isle of Man agency

04 Contribution from a Research Council

05 Contribution from the Department of Health or a Regional Health Authority

06 Overseas student award from the UK Government or the British Council

07 Contribution from a Training Agency

08 Other UK government award

09 Contribution from an overseas agency, government, university or industry

10 Contribution from UK industry or commerce

90 Other source of finance

99 Not known.

The majority of UK and European Union applicants will find themselves in category 02. It is your *eligibility for assessment* for a local authority (or SAAS or Northern Ireland Education and Library Board) award that counts, so you should enter 02 even if you expect that your parents' or spouse's income will be too high for you to receive assistance. Only enter 01 if you are sure you will be funding the entire cost of your tuition fees from your own private finance and are *not eligible* for a local authority/SAAS/Northern Ireland Education and Library Board Award.

There is space provided in the application (under **Student support arrangements**) for you to enter which body will assess your eligibility for funds. This is usually your LA (eg Leicestershire LA) if you are from England and Wales, or your Board (eg North Eastern Area) if you are from Northern Ireland, or SAAS if you are from Scotland. If you didn't enter 02 as your fee code, then enter whichever source of finance applies to you (eg sponsorship). It is possible to enter 'I prefer not to say'.

At the time of application, you may not be clear whether or not sponsorship will actually be awarded to you, and you may be applying to a number of companies at the same time. In this case, indicate the name of your first-choice sponsor. If the outcome of the application for sponsorship affects your year of entry, apply initially for 2008 entry, but indicate in your statement (see **Chapter 17**) that you might subsequently wish to defer to 2009 entry.

For more information on funding and other financial concerns, see **Chapter 3**.

Mailings from UCAS

UCAS may from time to time send out information not directly related to your application, but covering areas of interest such as funding, sponsorship opportunities, health issues, career possibilities relevant to your chosen subjects and goods/services (such as student banking and travel discounts) relevant to higher education. Please note that at no time are details of individual applicants released to any of the companies wishing to have information passed to you. Such information may be sent by email, text message or post. You should tick the relevant boxes if you wish to receive these mailings.

NOMINATED ACCESS

You can optionally name one person who can act on your behalf regarding your application. It is a good idea to do so, in case of illness or injury, for example. You need to fill in their name and also their relationship to you.

CRIMINAL CONVICTIONS

To help the universities and colleges reduce the risk of harm or injury to their students caused by the criminal behaviour of other students, they must know about any relevant criminal convictions held by an applicant. This information must be entered in the **Criminal convictions** section of the **Personal Details** area.

Relevant criminal convictions are convictions for offences against the person, whether of a violent or sexual nature, and convictions for offences involving unlawfully supplying controlled drugs or substances where the conviction concerns commercial drug dealing or trafficking. Convictions that are spent (as defined by the Rehabilitation of Offenders Act 1974) are not considered to be relevant and you should not reveal them.

You must tick the box if either of the following statements applies to you:

- I have a relevant criminal conviction that is not spent.
- I am serving a prison sentence for a relevant criminal conviction. (If you are currently serving a prison sentence for a relevant criminal conviction, then you must also give the prison address as your postal address on your application and a senior prison officer must support your application.)

If you tick the box, you will not be automatically excluded from the application process. However, the university or college concerned may want to consider the application further or ask for more information before making a decision.

You should be aware that for courses in teaching, health, social work, veterinary medicine, veterinary science or courses involving work with children or vulnerable adults, any criminal convictions, including sentences and cautions (including verbal cautions), reprimands, final warnings and bind-over orders are exempt from the Rehabilitation of Offenders Act 1974.

If you are applying for these courses, the universities and colleges will ask you to agree to have a criminal record check. You may also need an *enhanced disclosure document* from the Criminal Records Bureau or the Scottish

Criminal Record Office Disclosure Service. This means that if the criminal record check identifies that you have had a conviction, this information will be made available to the university or college considering your application.

The university or college will send you the appropriate documents to fill in. Where this document comes from will depend on where you are applying. You might find the details below useful:

- **England and Wales:** Criminal Records Bureau, www.crb.gov.uk
- **Scotland:** Scottish Criminal Record Office Disclosure Service, www.disclosurescotland.co.uk.

If you are convicted of a relevant criminal offence after you have applied, you must tell both UCAS and any university or college that you have applied to (or may apply to during the application cycle).

Do not send details of the offence; simply tell UCAS and the universities and colleges that you have a relevant criminal conviction. The universities and colleges may then ask you for more details.

Notes:

1 | Applicants or their advisers who wish to declare additional material information but do not wish to do so in their UCAS application should write directly to admissions officers at the institutions listed on their form or at any other institution considering their application.
2 | False information will include any inaccurate or omitted examination results.
3 | Omission of material information will include failure to complete correctly the declaration on the application relating to criminal convictions and failure to declare any other information which might be significant to your ability to commence or complete a course of study.

DISABILITY/SPECIAL NEEDS

Universities and colleges welcome students with disabilities and will try to meet their needs wherever they reasonably can. The information you give in the application will help them do this. UCAS will also use it to monitor progress in equal opportunities in higher education.

If you have a disability, special needs (including dyslexia or another specific learning difficulty) or a medical condition, you should select the most appropriate option from the list below. If you do not have a disability, special needs or a medical condition, select 'None'.

- None.
- You have a specific learning difficulty (for example, dyslexia).
- You are blind or partially sighted.
- You are deaf or hard of hearing.
- You use a wheelchair or have mobility difficulties.
- You have an autistic spectrum disorder or Asperger's syndrome.
- You have mental health difficulties.
- You have a disability that cannot be seen (for example, diabetes, epilepsy or a heart condition).
- You have two or more of the above.
- You have a disability, special needs or a medical condition that is not listed above.

Further information on these options (including case studies) is given on Apply.

A space is given for you to provide details of the disabilities, special needs or medical conditions that may affect you. Some applicants are reluctant to fill this in – either because they do not want to draw attention to themselves or because they think their chances of acceptance may be adversely affected. This is not the case. Institutions need to know about any measures they may need to take to cope effectively with your needs, and if you supply this information it will help them make suitable preparations – so that they can:

- Make necessary allowances (for example, they may be willing to lower entry requirements to allow for serious difficulties; they may need to provide you with readers or interpreters, or give you extra time to complete your course).
- Ensure that any additional facilities or equipment is available (for example, adapted accommodation).

It is in your interests to give all relevant information in this section. It will *not* affect the universities' and colleges' decisions regarding your suitability for the course.

If you claim special consideration on account of dyslexia, be prepared to provide independent evidence (usually, a psychologist's report). Admissions tutors will need to be convinced that you can keep up with the required work.

Finally, tick 'section completed' and click save to save all the information entered in **Personal Details** before moving on to the next section.

13

ADDITIONAL INFORMATION

This section of the application only appears if you answered 'Yes' to your permanent home being in the UK. It covers:

- Ethnic origin
- National identity
- Activities in preparation for higher education
- Occupational background
- Whether you have been in care
- Parental education
- Whether you would like to receive correspondence in Welsh.

Do not worry about this part of the application. It is designed to help UCAS and the universities and colleges monitor applications and equal opportunities, not to inform them during the selection process.

ETHNIC ORIGIN

You are asked to state your ethnic origin, or the category which broadly corresponds with the origin of your recent forebears: read the options in the dropdown list carefully, and then select one. The options are:

- White
- Black – Caribbean
- Black – African
- Black – Other background
- Asian – Indian

- Asian – Pakistani
- Asian – Bangladeshi
- Asian – Chinese
- Asian – Other background
- Mixed – White and Black Caribbean
- Mixed – White and Black African
- Mixed – White and Asian
- Mixed – Other background
- Other ethnic background
- I prefer not to say.

You *must* enter one of the options listed, even if it is 'I prefer not to say', or you will not be able to register your application as finished.

NATIONAL IDENTITY

You will be asked to classify your national identity. This is different from ethnicity and nationality and can be based on many things including, for example, culture, language or ancestry/family history.

You will need to describe your national identity using the options listed below. You can use either one option, for example 'Welsh', or two options if you feel you have dual national identity, for example 'English' and 'Scottish', or 'Irish' and 'Other' if you are Irish with a national identity not listed. If you feel that you have more than two national identities, you should select 'Other' for one or both options.

- British
- English
- Irish
- Scottish
- Welsh
- Other
- I prefer not to say
- Unknown
- Not applicable/not required.

ACTIVITIES IN PREPARATION FOR HIGHER EDUCATION

Summer schools and similar courses are held throughout the year and are also known as Saturday university, campus days, summer academies and booster courses. If you have taken part in one of these (or anything similar), select the relevant option and give more details of what you did in your personal statement.

You can enter up to two such activities in this section. If you have attended more than two summer schools, enter the most recent two. If you are unsure which option to select for the summer school you attended, ask your school or college adviser or refer to the website for guidance.

For each activity you have attended, enter its type using the options below:

- **HEFCE Regional**: www.hefce.ac.uk/widen/summsch
- **HEFCE National Specialist**: www.hefce.ac.uk/widen/summsch
- **NAGTY** – National Academy for Gifted & Talented Youth: www.nagty.ac.uk
- **Sutton Trust**: www.suttontrust.com
- **Scotland**: Includes Saturday university, campus days and summer academies for S1–S4, longer summer schools or booster courses for S5 and S6, summer activities aimed at general preparation or subject enhancement for mature applicants and preparation/bridging summer schools for applicants who want to progress from an HND to year 3 degree entry
- **Wales**: Includes summer schools run at Welsh universities for pupils from schools and colleges in Wales (see www.lamp.ac.uk/summeruni and www.swan.ac.uk/dace/dace2/en/rhrw.asp)
- **Northern Ireland**: Includes summer schools run at universities in Northern Ireland such as the Step-Up programme (www.ulster.ac.uk/stepup) and the Science Shop (www.ulster.ac.uk/scienceshop)
- **Other**: Any other summer schools, including taster courses, which are not mentioned in the list and which do not involve a cost to the individual.

Select the month and year that you attended the summer school from the dropdown lists, then select the number of days that you attended the course.

 If you attended a summer school which spanned more than one month, enter the month in which the summer school began.

OCCUPATIONAL BACKGROUND

Here you are asked to give the occupation of the parent or other person who brings the highest income into the home in which you have been brought up. Universities and colleges (and also government and researchers) need to know about the demand for higher education from within the various socioeconomic groups and how well that demand is being satisfied. For example, now that the student loans system means that students have to fund their study from their own money, it is important to know whether this is having an effect on demand and take-up of higher education among less well-off families.

CARE

The universities and colleges may be able to offer extra resources or support, for example with out-of-term accommodation, for those who have been in care at some stage. Choose 'Yes' if you have ever been in care, even for one day.

PARENTAL EDUCATION

You will be asked to indicate whether or not any of your parents, step-parents or guardians have any higher education qualifications, such as degrees, diplomas or certificates of higher education. If you are unsure, select 'Don't know' from the dropdown list. If you do not wish to disclose this information, you may select 'I prefer not to say'.

CORRESPONDENCE IN WELSH

If you have applied to one or more universities or colleges in Wales and you want them to correspond with you in Welsh, select 'Yes'. Note that you need to do this even if your whole application is in Welsh. Also note that UCAS will always correspond with you in English.

Since this section is only viewed by UK residents, other applicants unfortunately do not have the opportunity to use Apply to request correspondence in Welsh. If you are in this position, you need to make requests directly to the relevant instititutions.

Finally, tick 'section completed' and click save to save all the information entered in Additional Information before moving on to the next section.

14

CHOICES

This is one of the most important parts of your application, representing the culmination of your research into higher education. As such, it is often best to leave entering details of the courses you are applying to until you have completed all the factual information required, and worked out your personal statement.

Specifically, this section covers:

- Previous applications
- Institution code
- Course code
- Campus code
- Start date
- Further details
- Living at home
- Point of entry
- Art and design courses.

You are allowed a maximum of five course applications, which should be obvious in light of the space provided. You can apply to fewer than five if you wish, and can add other courses until the end of June (12 June for Art & Design Route B applications). If you applied to only one course initially you will be allowed to add up to four additional choices, but only if you pay the difference between the single and multiple application fees (£5 and £15 respectively – see **Chapter 18** for more information).

PREVIOUS APPLICATIONS

You will be asked for your previous application number before you complete the **Choices** section in Apply. Type in your previous application number or, if you cannot remember it, leave the box blank.

If you have applied before, do not try to hide the fact. Indeed, it may help if the universities and colleges can identify your previous application, especially if they made you an offer you failed to achieve. They can look up their interview records or their previous notes on your application, and may decide to give you another chance. (Do be aware, however, that some admissions tutors do not consider retake candidates and some will make higher offers – see **Chapter 10.**)

INSTITUTION CODE

To make it absolutely clear which courses you are applying to, you need to include details both of the courses and of the institutions that run them. Apply gives you the option of entering these details using course and institution names or codes. You can either find the relevant code using the **Course Search** area of the UCAS website, or find the relevant institution name using Apply. If you opt for the latter method, click on **see list**; this will bring up an alphabetical list from which you can select the relevant code(s) by the name of the *institution(s)* to which you wish to apply.

COURSE CODE

As before, you can find out the code for the course you wish to enter via the UCAS website or by clicking **see list** next to the relevant space in Apply and selecting your course from the alphabetical list that appears (only courses offered at your chosen institution will be displayed for you to select from).

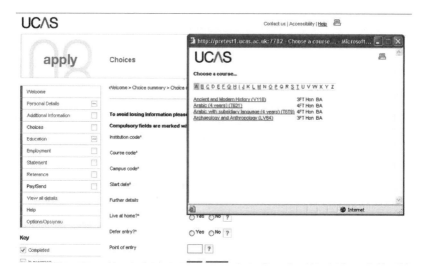

Apply will bring up an error message if you enter a course code that is not recognised, but it is still possible to apply to a course unintentionally if you do not double-check that the code you enter corresponds to the course that interests you. Make sure you have access to course information (such as on the UCAS website) and click **save** after each entry. This helps you check for any mistakes.

>
> Do not forget that you can make insurance subject choices as alternatives to your applications to medicine, dentistry or veterinary science (see Chapter 8).

CAMPUS CODE

Some courses are taught at franchised institutions, ie away from the main university or college. If this is the case for one of your chosen courses, you will need to enter a campus code (for example, the Carlisle campus of the University of Northumbria is represented by the letter C). Enter the relevant code by clicking on **see list** next to the campus code column. If you are not sure whether a campus code is needed, you can click on **save** and see whether Apply highlights the campus box to be filled in. Even if your course is only available at one campus, you may need to select *main site* from the list.

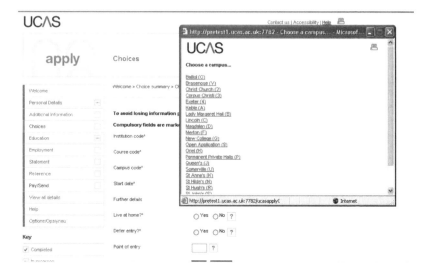

START DATE

A list of available start dates will be displayed when you click on **see list**. If you want to apply at this stage for deferred entry (that is, starting your course in 2009 rather than 2008), you should select the correct date from the list. More information on deferred entry is given in **Chapter 8**. Your personal statement (see **Chapter 17**) gives you the chance to explain why it is that you want to defer entry.

It is no use applying for 2009 entry in 2007–8 if some of your exams will be taken in 2008–9. Even though your admission is deferred, a final decision on this application has to be taken by August 2008. Furthermore, you are not allowed to keep a deferred place at a university or college and then apply the following year to other institutions of the same kind. UCAS has ways of intercepting such applications!

FURTHER DETAILS

On many UCAS applications this part is left empty. But further information may be requested by institutions and should be provided. Check the course search facility on the UCAS website or the university or college prospectus to find out whether this is the case. The sort of information you may need to give could include:

- The duration of the course (three- or four-year course)
- Minor, subsidiary or first-year course option choice
- Specialisations within your chosen course
- Qualified Teacher Status
- Previous applications
- If you are applying to Oxford and have selected a permanent private hall (rather than a college with a campus code) then this section can be used to state which hall you have chosen.

LIVING AT HOME

If you are planning to live at home while attending a particular university or college, click in the relevant tick box marked 'Yes'. This information is unlikely to make a difference to your chances of acceptance but may help institutions plan their accommodation requirements. If you are not planning to live at home, leave the box blank.

POINT OF ENTRY

If you plan to join the course at the beginning of the first year then leave this part blank. If you think you may qualify for credit transfer or *entry with advanced standing* (entry at second-year level or perhaps third-year level in Scotland) you should check this possibility with the institutions to which you wish to apply before completing your application. You may then indicate this to the universities and colleges by entering 2 or 3 (ie the year of proposed entry) in the relevant box for each application to which this is relevant.

ART AND DESIGN COURSES

As explained in **Chapter 8**, there are two routes for application to art and design courses. If you wish to apply for courses via Route A (simultaneous) you do so by indicating your choices in the usual way, outlined above. If you are completing an art and design Route A entry, you will be asked whether you want to apply through Route B (sequential) later on – respond to this by ticking the relevant box. You will then be able to add your Route B choices later on Track.

Remember that you are only allowed to apply for five courses, *including* any through Route B. This means that if you tick the Route B box you can only apply to a maximum of four further courses in the usual manner. As explained in **Chapter 8**, you can freely mix and match your courses both in art and design and other subjects. The only constraint is that you have a maximum of three choices in Route B, all of which must be art and design courses as indicated by the UCAS website. You will be given the opportunity to supply an amended personal statement for your Route B applications, but be aware that, should you decide to apply to a range of art and design and non-art and design courses through Route A, you will need to justify this in your main personal statement (see **Chapter 17**).

15

EDUCATION

It is essential that you include information about your education to date in your application. This helps to give institutions a better idea of who you are, as well as providing them with evidence of your academic attainment and potential. They will, of course, also use the information you give here to put together conditional offers.

Specifically, this section covers:

■ Schools and colleges attended
■ Qualifications (already attained and yet to be taken).

SCHOOLS AND COLLEGES ATTENDED

Apply will ask you to add details for the schools and colleges that you have attended (including overseas). You must enter at least one school or college. Click on **add a school/college** and use the **find** button to search for your institution; the centre number will be entered automatically. Higher education and overseas institutions do not usually have centre numbers, so if you have studied at one you will need to leave the centre number box blank. A warning will appear asking you to enter a number, but you can still move on to the next screen to continue your application.

Enter all of the secondary schools, colleges and universities you have attended, up to a maximum of ten. If you have attended more than this, enter the most recent ten. If you have spent any time at a higher education institution you must say so, and be prepared for questions about it should you be called for interview.

If you cannot find your school, click on **My school/centre is not listed here**. You can then type the name of the school directly into the box. Select the dates you attended from the dropdown lists. You will also need to enter the centre number. You can obtain this from your school or by looking on your examination certificates.

If you have been home-schooled for all of your secondary education, click on **find** and enter a term such as *home*. If a suitable option is not there, click on **My school/centre is not listed here** and then type *home-schooled* directly into the box.

 Mature students should complete this section as fully as possible – many forget to list their present college.

QUALIFICATIONS

As outlined in **Chapter 6**, this part of the application is crucial as it is bound to be examined carefully by admissions tutors. There are so many different kinds of qualifications that you may already have, or be planning to take, that it is also a potentially confusing area – you need to take care that you include all the relevant information as outlined below.

ENTERING YOUR QUALIFICATIONS

After entering the details of the schools and colleges you have attended, you will be presented with a list of them and a link beneath each one called 'add a qualification'. Check that everything (dates of attendance etc) is in order and click on **add a qualification** to enter the qualifications that you took at that school or college. The link will take you through to a list of qualifications that your school/college teaches, for example:

- A level
- A level double award
- GCSE
- GCSE double award
- European Baccalaureate.

If your qualification is not listed, you can click on **Other qualification type not in this list** to access an A to Z list of qualifications. Click on a qualification that you have taken (or will be taking – see below). This will take you through to a screen where you can enter all the details of the qualification. For example, for a GCSE you will need to enter the subject, date of examination, awarding body, grade and centre (school/college) at which you took/will be taking it. If you have not yet completed a qualification, leave the grade box as *pending*. You will also be asked to enter information about the units you have taken and unit grades you have achieved in qualifications which have been completed and certificated such as GCE AS levels.

Once you have completed this screen you then have the option to add another subject for that particular qualification. When you have no more subjects to add, click save. At this point, if anything is amiss, you will be told by the green text. If everything is in order, you will be shown the qualifications and subjects you have already entered and given the option to 'add' another qualification. Click on this if you have anything to add and start the process again.

Once you have entered all the qualifications you have completed or are yet to complete, tick 'section completed' and click save. If you have entered a vocational qualification or Scottish qualification, you will be prompted to enter your BTEC registration number or Scottish candidate number in the relevant box. Ask your college if you do not know your number. This information could be very important if there is any delay in getting your results to a university or college where you are holding an offer – it could mean the difference between landing a place and losing it.

You can return to the Education area of your application to edit or add to the entries already made, up to the point when you submit your application through your Apply coordinator.

WHICH QUALIFICATIONS TO INCLUDE?

QUALIFICATIONS YOU HAVE ALREADY RECEIVED
You should list *all* qualifications for which you have received certification from the awarding body (this will usually include GCSEs, Scottish Standard Grades and Intermediate Awards, Intermediate GNVQs and so on). Include all the qualifications you have taken, even if you didn't pass them. **You must not conceal anything because, at a later stage, you will have to declare that you have entered complete and accurate information.** You may be asked to supply original certificates to support the qualifications listed in your application at any time during the application process. You must include details of these qualifications even if you are planning to retake, whether completely or only in part. (You can explain your reasons for retaking in your personal statement.)

If you are an **A level student**, you must include all GCE AS qualifications for which you have been awarded a grade that you have *not* declined, ie all those that have been certificated. You must also include your unit grades. If you have opted to decline a result you should only include that qualification in your application if you intend to retake, treating it as a qualification yet to be taken. You must also include individual units that do not form part of a full qualification (eg Free-standing Mathematics Qualification) and for which you have accepted certification.

If you are a **mature student** with no formal qualifications, enter *no formal qualifications* on the application and see page 124 for advice on how you can address this in your personal statement. If you are hoping to enter university or college via the Accreditation of Prior Learning (APL) or the Accreditation of Prior Experiential Learning (APEL), you should contact your chosen institution before applying to UCAS (see page 41).

If you are an **international student**, you need to give full details of all your qualifications in the original language. Do not try to provide a UK equivalent. If your first language is not English, but your qualifications were completely or partly assessed in English, make this clear. You should also provide details of any English language tests you have taken or plan to take, giving dates, titles and any syllabus codes. Send a copy of all transcripts, certificates or other proof of your qualifications direct to each university or college you apply to, quoting the title and code number of the course and your UCAS application number. Do not, however, send anything of this sort to UCAS.

QUALIFICATIONS YOU ARE STUDYING FOR
You must also enter details of all qualifications that you are studying for now and those for which you are awaiting results. These may include A levels, Scottish Highers and Advanced Highers, BTEC qualifications, NVQs, Access courses and so on.

QUALIFICATIONS SUMMARY

With Apply, it is relatively easy to know what to include because the qualifications are all there, ready for you to choose from. However, a list of the full range of English, Scottish and International qualifications is provided below to give you an overview. Where a qualification is relatively new, its old 'equivalent' is indicated – if this is what you have, include it.

ENGLISH, WELSH AND NORTHERN IRISH QUALIFICATIONS
- GCSE (include short course GCSE and vocational GCSE)
- GCE AS level
- GCE A level
- GCE Advanced Extension Award
- BTEC National and Higher National Diplomas or Certificates (eg ND, HND, HNC)
- Welsh Baccalaureate Advanced Diploma
- National Vocational Qualifications or NVQs
- Apprenticeship/Advanced Apprenticeship (incorporating NVQs)
- Key Skills qualifications
- Free-standing Mathematics Qualification
- Access to Higher Education courses
- Diploma in Foundation Studies (art and design)
- Open College Networks
- Music, drama and dance qualifications (eg ABRSM, LAMDA, RAD – only list your highest grade)
- Open University qualifications
- Other higher education qualifications.

SCOTTISH QUALIFICATIONS
- Standard Grades
- Intermediate 1
- Intermediate 2
- Highers
- Advanced Highers

■ National Units
■ National Certificate modules
■ SCE Short Courses
■ Scottish Group Awards
■ Other Group Awards (HNC, HND, PDA, SVQ, SPA, GSVQ, National Certificate Clusters, School Group Awards)
■ Core Skills Profile
■ Access programmes (SWAP).

Tip	If you have one, you should take your full Progress File (a record of your personal development, skills development and achievements) with you if invited for interview. If you wish, send a brief summary (not the full record) direct to the institution, quoting your application number. You should be prepared to discuss and explain what your Progress File comprises, and how it was developed.

16

EMPLOYMENT

It is very useful for admissions tutors to know if you have had a job or under-taken work shadowing or work experience. This can be particularly helpful if you have worked in an area relevant to your application or chosen career. Full-time and part-time jobs (including weekend ones) are worth including, but only if they have been continued for a reasonable period. Even if the jobs you held were just to earn pocket money, an admissions tutor will see this as a broadening of your experience. Note that institutions undertake *not* to contact previous employers for a reference without your permission.

If you have information to enter, click on **add an employer** in the **Employment** area of Apply. Then fill in the employer's name and address, job details, start and end dates and whether it is/was full or part time. If the job you are entering is where you are currently employed, then you do not need to enter a date under 'When did you finish?'. Click **save** to take you to the employment summary screen and then – when you are ready – tick 'section completed' and click **save**.

If you do not have anything to enter in this section, you just need to tick 'section completed' and click **save**.

17

PERSONAL STATEMENT

This section is crucial because it is the *only* part of the application where you have the chance to select and emphasise points about yourself, and explain to admissions officers why you are interested in your chosen subjects. Personal statements submitted via Apply have a maximum length of 4000 characters (47 lines) – so you need to think very carefully about exactly what you want to say in the limited space provided. You can click on save at any time to update the line count.

WHAT ARE THE ADMISSIONS TUTORS LOOKING FOR?

FACTUAL INFORMATION
The admissions tutors will want to know about:

- Your career aspirations.
- Your reasons for choosing the course(s).
- Relevant background or experience, which may include work experience/work shadowing, practical activity in music or theatre, attendance on courses, time abroad etc. Evidence of practical experience may be vital to the success of an application to a medical or veterinary school, and may also significantly assist if you are applying for some management and engineering courses.
- Any interests you may have (eg Duke of Edinburgh's award, charity fundraising, painting, potholing, positions of responsibility). These may not seem strictly relevant to the course, but they help to give an impression of you as a person.

■ The name of any sponsor you may have. Relatively few students are sponsored through their courses and you will not be at a disadvantage if you have nothing to include in this respect. Institutions are keen to know, however, if you have been able to secure this form of financial support. If you have applied for sponsorship but do not yet know whether you have been successful, say where you have applied to.

> It is difficult for an applicant who has selected a wide range of disparate courses to give feasible reasons for having done so, which is why this approach is not recommended.

READING BETWEEN THE LINES

Your statement will convey more about you than just the facts. The way you present them will give valuable clues about other qualities such as critical thinking and communication skills.

ANALYTICAL SKILLS

Admissions tutors are usually looking for students who can analyse their current experience. A common weakness is that applicants tend to describe what they are doing now rather than analysing their current experiences, relating them to what they hope to get from higher education and future career prospects.

Alongside the descriptive approach tends to go a listing of data already entered in the application (ie present studies) or details of apparently unrelated hobbies. Hobbies *are* an important part of your statement, but they need to be analysed in the context of how they have contributed to your skills or personal development in a way that would support success on the courses to which you have applied.

COMMUNICATION SKILLS

The text and presentation of your statement provides the admissions tutor with an indication of your communication skills — both in terms of basic grammar and spelling and in terms of your ability to express information and ideas clearly.

MATURITY

A good statement provides evidence of maturity of thought and a sense of responsibility. If you intend to study away from home, it is important to show that you have these attributes, as they indicate that you will be likely to adapt well to your new environment.

Top tips

- **Impression**: Think about the impression you want to give – you need to make yourself sound interesting, bright, mature and eager to learn.

- **Structure**: Organise what you want to say into a logical structure and make sure everything you say is clear and concise. Use subheadings if you think it will help.

- **Length**: Do not try to pack too much in – it can get confusing. Hit the reader with your main point, and *do not* worry about filling up all 47 lines – rambling on simply to use all the space is likely to be counterproductive.

- **Relevance**: You should explain *why* each point you mention is relevant. Do not unnecessarily repeat material that already appears on the application form.

- **Honesty**: It is imperative that you be honest and specific. If necessary, be selective – there are only 24 hours in a day, and claiming too much is not always a good idea.

- **Accuracy**: Check the spelling – Apply does not have spellcheck facilities. It is therefore recommended that you word-process your statement as a Word document and spellcheck it first, before cutting and pasting it into the relevant Apply area. Get someone else to read it through, too – as it's sometimes hard to spot your own mistakes, and computer spellcheckers are not infallible.

- **Placing 'leads'**: Admissions tutors are likely to use your statement as a source of questions if they call you for interview. You should therefore only mention things you are prepared to talk about at an interview. If there is something you would particularly like to be asked to discuss, you can give the interviewer a 'lead' by mentioning it in your statement.

and finally...

- **Check up on yourself**: Read through everything you have written critically. Try to imagine *you* were the admissions tutor, trying to pick holes in what you have written. You may also find it useful to work with friends – read through each other's drafts – you will be surprised how often a friend will say to you 'but haven't you forgotten your...'

Tip Save your work regularly to keep the line count updated, and click to **preview** your statement. Click **edit** to make changes, and tick 'section completed' and click **save** to complete.

CREATING A WINNING STATEMENT

Amazingly, every year there are a few applicants who leave the Statement section completely blank. Obviously this is inadvisable to say the least! But many others do themselves no good simply as a result of the way they present information. The best way to illustrate the pitfalls is by using real examples...

Example 1

> Reading, knitting, walking.

Comment
Is this really all you have to say? You do not have to be Einstein to realise that this personal statement is woefully inadequate.

Example 2

> I have been interested in accounting for quite a long time and that's been one of the reasons I took Accounts at GCSE. I was hoping to do Accounts at A level but it was not available at my school. I have had some experience in accounting during Year 10 at school. I found a placement at Electrolux Accounts Department for a week and enjoyed it very much. We were unable to do work experience in Year 12 due to insurance problems. I think the career prospects are good for accounting with many rewards.
>
> I am quite active and enjoy sports like squash, tennis, football and golf. My main sport is golf and I am a member of the local golf club playing off a handicap of 15. I represented my school at golf last year at Seaton Carew and hope to play again this year.

Comment
This was an attempt to do it properly, and there are a few useful points, but the general impression is superficial and negative – it seems that the applicant has simply wandered into accounting as a choice without giving it any serious thought, and the casual tone of the writing does not create a good impression. On the other hand, at least he or she has been specific about their

sporting interests: too many people just write 'reading' or 'music'. And, it is accurately spelt – such things matter.

Example 3

> At present, I am secretary of the social committee for Years 12 and 13 which arranges social events and also attempts to improve facilities. I have held the position of house captain and also been involved with various sports teams and subject-related clubs.
>
> After abandoning my childhood dream of becoming an astronaut, I became drawn towards the legal profession. Subsequently my work experience in Year 11 was at one of Sheffield's largest solicitors. During the two weeks I was there I spent a brief time in Commercial, Matrimonial and Police Prosecution departments. All these aspects of law were interesting but my experience in the Criminal Law department was very stimulating and this is the area I wish to pursue a career in – ultimately in the capacity of a barrister.
>
> Outside of school, I am also a member of a sub-aqua branch helping in most aspects of the club, especially the maintenance and administration of equipment and the training (theoretical and practical) of other members. I am a keen cyclist and tennis player and my other interests lie in modern cinema and horology. I also enjoy two part-time jobs where my duties range from gardening, labouring and driving, to shopkeeping, stocktaking and the use of an electronic till.

Comment

This is a much stronger statement – note the much more convincing justification for the choice of course; a selector would feel that thought had gone into this. It might have been better to put the second paragraph first – you should try to organise your statement into themed sections covering:

■ Career aspirations
■ Reasons for course choice and interest in subject
■ Academic interests
■ Details of any exams results/achievements you have not entered elsewhere in your UCAS application (eg Duke of Edinburgh's Award, Millennium Volunteers, Young Enterprise)
■ Extra-curricular interests and achievements
■ Work experience.

> **Tip**
>
> If you want to supply more information than the **Statement** space allows, send it direct to your chosen universities or colleges. (Do not send it to UCAS.)

Example 4

I believe that sciences are the key to the future development of the nation and I intend to be a part of this – that is why I have chosen to study Chemistry at university.

My passion for science has been reinforced by the work experience I have had in the area: my Saturday job at a local pharmacy made me aware of the enormous amount of research going on into developing new drugs to treat illnesses. I pursued this interest by spending two weeks work-shadowing a lab assistant at a major pharmaceuticals company.

During my early school career I held various positions of responsibility: I was my form's representative on the school council for three years and, in Year 11, I was appointed prefect.

In the sixth form I have been elected senior student. This post involves many responsibilities, including attending functions such as a meeting with the President of Lithuania. As a student councillor I have been responsible for the production of the annual yearbook.

I am also an active member in the college charities group. We have held karaoke sessions in the lunch hours, and non-uniform days; in total we have raised over £4000. Outside college I work in a local soup kitchen for the homeless.

I have recently been elected to represent the youth of Blackpool on the Blackpool Police and Community Forum.

I take an active interest in sports – I am a member of the basketball team, a sport in which I have taken a refereeing course. I was also the school discus champion.

Comment

This example is even tauter, and says everything that needs saying clearly and concisely. This applicant realises that they are applying for competitive courses, and set out to sell themselves – without going over the top. It would have been even better if the candidate had mentioned something specific that interested them about their work experience or their A level course, as this would give the admissions tutor a useful 'lead' at interview.

SPECIFIC ADVICE

The personal statement is especially important in subjects like **creative and performing arts**. Say what you have done, seen or heard – do not be one of the music applicants who does not actually mention their chosen instrument!

Applicants for **teacher-training, medicine, veterinary science, dentistry** or **physiotherapy** courses should be sure to give details of work experience (including locations and dates).

If you are currently studying for a **vocational or occupational qualification** with which admissions tutors may be relatively unfamiliar, explain the relevance of your studies to the course(s) for which you are applying.

If you are an **international student**, explain *why* you want to study in the UK. Can you provide evidence that you will be able to complete a course delivered in English?

If you are a **sporting** person, give details of your achievements. 'I play tennis' adds little; 'I play tennis for the county' shows that you are committed to something you excel in.

If you plan to take a **gap year** it is advisable to cover your reasons for doing so in your statement. Remember that anything you say is likely to be used as a basis for questions at interview. The two examples below show common pitfalls:

Example 1

> In my gap year I hope to work and travel.

Comment
This statement is far too vague, and would cause many admissions tutors to wonder whether you had really good reasons for deferring entry, or whether you were just postponing the decision to take up a place on their course.

Example 2

> I have applied for deferred entry in order to gain work experience and then visit New Zealand.

Comment

This is likely to lead to questions such as: What kind of work experience? For how long? Is it relevant to your chosen course? How? Why New Zealand? What will you do while you are there? Try to be as specific – this candidate's statement would have been better if they had explained why they wanted work experience and what drew them to New Zealand.

MATURE STUDENTS

You should say something about what you have done since leaving school. If, like many mature applicants, you are rather older and have had a variety of occupations and experience, you may find the Apply screens too restrictive. In this case you can, if you wish, summarise your career and then send a full CV direct to your chosen institutions (*not* to UCAS). However, there is enough space for you to present your background and interests in fair detail. Everyone's circumstances are different, but the following example is the kind of thing that might attract an admissions tutor's favourable attention.

1973	Left school aged 16, no qualifications
1974–79	Various periods of travel, manual work and unemployment
1979–87	RAF (included technical training)
1987–2000	Self-employed (motor repairs)
2001–03	Access course, Silverbridge College (full-time) with a view to entering Law School

Most of my experience has been in manual trades, but I now think I have the ability to change direction. I have known many people who have taken degrees and I think I can make a success of it. My interest in law was awakened by a friend's problem over an insurance claim. I tried to help her and started exploring the law books in the library. I realised that this was an intellectual challenge I could relate to. Since then I have done more reading and visited the courts. I have started to help in the Citizens' Advice Bureau. Now I want to qualify and I hope to work in a Community Law Centre. My non-academic interests include travel (in various countries), motor car restoration and socialising.

18

FINISHING OFF

DECLARATION

The declaration can be found under the **send to referee** section of Apply. Once you have completed all sections of Apply, you need to read the declaration carefully, only agreeing if you are absolutely sure that you are happy with its content. UCAS cannot process your application unless you confirm your agreement with their terms and conditions, which legally binds you to make the required payment (see page 126).

When you submit your application, there is no need to sign anything by hand: ticking the relevant boxes and clicking on the **I agree** button suffices. Remember, by agreeing you are saying that the information you have provided is accurate and complete and that you agree to abide by the rules of UCAS. You are also agreeing to your personal data being processed by UCAS and institutions under the relevant data protection legislation. Any offer of a place you may receive is made on the understanding that, in accepting it, you agree to abide by the rules and regulations of the institution.

In pursuance of the prevention of fraud, UCAS reserves the right to disclose information given in your application to outside agencies, for example the Police, the Home Office, Local Authorities, Examining Boards, the Department of Social Security or the Student Loans Company.

If UCAS or an institution has reason to believe that you or any other person has omitted any mandatory information requested in the instructions on Apply, has failed to include any additional material information, has made any misrepresentation or given false information, UCAS and/or the institution will take whatever steps it considers necessary to establish whether the information given in your application is correct. UCAS and the institutions reserve the right at any time to request that you, your referee or your employer provide further information relating to any part of your application, eg proof of identity, status, academic qualifications or employment history. If such information is not provided within the time limit set by UCAS, then UCAS reserves the right to cancel your application. Fees paid to UCAS in respect of applications that are cancelled as a result of failure to provide additional information as requested, or for providing fraudulent information, are not refundable.

SUBMITTING YOUR APPLICATION

Once you have agreed to the terms of the declaration you can pass your application on to your UCAS coordinator or administrator, who will usually be a head of sixth form, form teacher or careers adviser. They will then check it over, add your reference (see page 127), make arrangements for collecting your application fee and, finally, send it to UCAS.*

If you find that you need to alter your application after you have submitted it, you should ask your UCAS coordinator or administrator to return it to you. You will then be able to make the necessary changes before resubmitting it. You may find that mistakes are spotted by the coordinator/administrator themselves who will return it to you for amendments.

PAYMENT

Application to higher education via UCAS costs £15 (or £5 if you only apply to one course).

If you are making your application through your school or college, they will let you know how they handle payments. (Normally you will pay by debit card, but some schools and colleges prefer to collect individual applicants' fees themselves and send one large payment to UCAS covering everyone). If you are *not* making your application through your school or college you will need to make your payment via the internet using a credit or debit card.

You do not need to make your payment until you have completed your application. Once you have agreed to the terms of use of the Apply system in the

*If you are using Apply as an individual rather than via a school or college, you are responsible for entering your own reference, and submitting your application direct to UCAS.

Declaration, you will be asked for your card details (if you are paying by this method). Apply will automatically know whether you should pay the full £15 or the single choice fee of £5.

UCAS accepts Visa, Delta, MasterCard, Maestro (UK-issued only), Solo and Visa Electron (UK-issued only) credit and debit cards. At the moment they do not accept American Express, JCB cards or Maestro cards that have been issued outside the UK. The card you use to pay need not be in your own name but you will require the consent of the cardholder.

REFERENCE

The good news is that you do not have to write your own reference, so there is relatively little for you to do here. Your referee (usually a teacher, if you are applying via a school or college) will write it and then attach it to your application, via the UCAS administrator. Having said this, it is important not to disregard your reference entirely. It is in some ways the most important item in the selection process. It is only your referee who can tell the admissions tutor about your attitude and motivation, and who can comment on your ability, so that admissions tutors are not reliant solely on the exam results and information about exams to be taken that you provide elsewhere in your application.

Points of particular concern to admissions tutors include:

- Academic achievement and potential
- Suitability and motivation for the chosen course
- Predicted grades
- Personal qualities
- Career aspirations.

Referees are asked to estimate your level of performance in forthcoming exams, and these predictions of likely grades are important to your chances of acceptance. The best advice, in this respect, is to work hard and impress your referee!

As a result of the Data Protection Act 1998, you have the right to see your reference. You should contact UCAS if you want to see what your referee has written about you. You will be charged a £10 handling fee to receive a copy. Unlike in previous years, there is now no such thing as a confidential reference.

Your reference will normally come from your present school or college, or the one you attended most recently. If you choose anyone else, make sure it is someone who can provide the kind of assessment higher education institutions need. Be aware that, if you are attending a school or college, it will look very odd if you choose someone from outside as your referee.

 On **no account** should your reference come from a relative.

If you find it impossible to nominate an academic referee, find someone who can at least comment objectively on your personal qualities, motivation and ability to cope with a degree or HND course. An application containing no reference will be held at UCAS until one is supplied.

WHAT HAPPENS NEXT?

On receipt of your application, usually within 24 hours, UCAS will mail out a welcome letter containing your applicant number and personal ID, plus a copy of the list of your higher education course choices. You should check this thoroughly and contact UCAS immediately if anything is incorrect.

You can use your application number to log on to Track in order to follow the progress of your application. Later in the application cycle you will receive instructions from UCAS that will help you to conclude a successful higher education application. For more information on this and on offers, see **Part II: The admissions procedure – applications, interviews, offers and beyond**.

19

TROUBLESHOOTING

I CANNOT LOG IN...
If your buzzword or password does not seem to be working, check the following:

- Have you entered the password correctly? Remember that login details are case-sensitive – check that you have all the characters exactly right
- Are you in the student area (not the staff area, which is for your referee)?
- Is your computer properly connected to the internet?
- Are you able to connect to other websites?

If the answer to all of these questions is 'Yes' then you may have a problem with your network or internet service provider (ISP). Try connecting to the main UCAS site www.ucas.com – if you can, there may be a problem with Apply and you should call UCAS's technical support on 01242 544683.

I'VE FORGOTTEN MY USERNAME/PASSWORD...
If you forget your username and password at any time, click on **Forgotten login?**, enter your name and date of birth and you will be presented with your chosen security questions. Should you answer correctly, the system will find you and you will be able to log in normally. Your username and password will be provided to you on the screen – make sure you write it down somewhere and keep it safe this time! Your UCAS coordinator does not hold it so it's up to you to remember it.

You can change your password and/or your security questions by clicking on **Options/Opsiynau** to the left of the screen.

I'M LOCKED OUT...

If you attempt to log on five times without success, for whatever reason, your account will automatically be locked. To regain access, you can...

- Click on **Forgotten login?** and, if you answer the security questions correctly, you will be able to enter the area.
- Ask the UCAS administrator at your centre to unlock your account and/or help create a new password for you.
- Call the UCAS Customer Service Unit for help, on 0871 468 0468.

Alternatively, you can wait for 24 hours – after which you will be able to try again.

Your account will also be locked if you close the internet browser window in which Apply is sitting, rather than exiting by logging out. If this happens, and you attempt to log back in, you will be presented with the following message:

> *You are already logged in. Please ensure this is your only active session. Click 'log in' if you wish to proceed.*

This is to protect against your application being open in more than one place at the same time. If you click on **log in** you will be allowed back into your account.

 Tip If you leave Apply open without touching it for an hour, it will time out for security reasons and you will have to log in again.

I'VE PASTED MY STATEMENT INTO APPLY AND IT'S ALL GONE WRONG...

The default character size for statements in Apply is 12 points. If you have written your personal statement in Word and used a smaller font size then it won't fit when you try to paste it into Apply, and you will have to reduce the length.

You may lose formatting and foreign characters when you paste your personal statement into Apply – you should edit your statement very carefully. You will not be able to use bold or italicised fonts.

I'VE COMPLETED MY APPLICATION AND SENT IT TO MY REFEREE, BUT NOW I WANT TO MAKE A CHANGE TO IT...

You'll have to email or personally contact your referee who can send the document back to you to amend.

MORE TROUBLE TO SHOOT?

Once you start completing your application, there is **help** to be accessed on each screen of Apply. Most difficulties can be quickly sorted by clicking on **Help** and following the clear instructions.

Alternatively, you can go to the **about Apply** section on the homepage of www.ucas.com.

AND FINALLY...

If you feel you need more information on the application process, UCAS provides a comprehensive list of useful publications on its website, www.ucasbooks.com.

PAPER APPLICATIONS

For 2007 entry, 99.7% of all applicants chose to apply online. UCAS understands that occasionally applicants do have a genuine need to submit a paper application. UCAS will continue to meet this demand on an individual basis: if you require a paper form, you should contact the Customer Service Unit on 0871 468 0468 and will need to explain why you need or wish to apply on paper. The adviser will then talk you through the process.

A NOTE FOR STAFF ON APPLY

The online UCAS application system, developed over the last few years, affords real benefits both to student applicants and to UCAS coordinators or administrators in schools, colleges or careers/Connexions centres.

Apply is a secure area of the UCAS website and no installation is necessary.

Students can use Apply to complete online UCAS applications at school, home or anywhere with internet access. When finished, they can send their applications to you for checking and to have references added, before you submit their applications to meet the relevant UCAS deadline.

The Apply system has dramatically reduced the number of errors made by applicants as they can access online help at every stage of completing their applications. Poor handwriting is consigned to the past. It is possible for personal statements to be checked and revised a number of times, as the information can be easily amended and kept up to date.

Also, Apply allows great flexibility in the mode of payment chosen by the centre. The fee payment method is variable and can be changed through the cycle of UCAS application.

As the UCAS administrator or coordinator, you will be posted a centre username and password with the June UCAS mailings to schools and other centres. You can then register with UCAS to use Apply – free of charge – by logging in and entering your name, details of your organisation and a unique buzzword of between 6 and 30 letters and numerals chosen by you, for use by your applicants. The buzzword identifies your centre to UCAS and will enable applicants to link through your centre to register with Apply.

Registration does not commit your centre to using Apply only.

Students employ the buzzword to register to use Apply, when their own username is generated. This must be written down and kept safe, as you will not know your applicants' usernames. They then decide on a password and four security questions.

As a UCAS coordinator, you will be in charge of staff set-up – registering appropriate staff with individual usernames and passwords. It is a simple task to remove, change or register new staff with different levels of administrative access (permissions).

From the **staff main area** you can access:

- **Applications** – showing all the applications being made from your centre, enabling you to view applications and check the progress of individuals
- **References** – where references can be written, read and approved
- **Send to UCAS** – where you can check the status of applications sent to the staff area, methods of payment, individual applicant fees, dates applications were sent to UCAS and students' application numbers (added to student records by UCAS, signifying that those applications have been received)
- **Delete applications** – where you can delete an applicant's record if it is no longer required
- **Security** – where it is possible to change students' passwords or security questions, and where accounts can be unlocked after unsuccessful login attempts
- **Setup** – containing all the standard details, your buzzword, chosen method(s) of payment and dates when your centre's applicants will be unavailable for interview, and where you can also register staff members' details and change their permissions
- **Options/Opsiynau** – where you can change the language presented in Apply to Welsh or back to English.

The Apply system is a useful administrative tool which can significantly cut the time spent by staff on the annual cycle of UCAS applications. It is worth gaining the support of senior management to introduce Apply and train other staff in its use. UCAS offers one-day training sessions for centre staff managing the Apply process.